THE TAKEOVER DIALOGUES

A DISCUSSION OF HOSTILE TAKEOVERS

EDMUND J. KELLY

Authors Choice Press
San Jose New York Lincoln Shanghai

The Takeover Dialogues
A Discussion of Hostile Takeovers

Authors Choice Press
an imprint of iUniverse.com, Inc.

For information address:
iUniverse.com, Inc.
5220 S 16th, Ste. 200
Lincoln, NE 68512
www.iuniverse.com

Originally published by Washington Network Press

ISBN: 0-595-16366-1

Printed in the United States of America

PUBLISHER'S FORWARD

Is a corporation just a legal entity, a paper value unit to be bought, sold and profited from by those shrewd enough to invest at the right time? Or is a corporation an important unit of society made up of people whose special training prepares them for the vital task of creating and maintaining capital? Do corporate raiders help a corporation reach its ultimate value, or does the raider's unwillingness to recognize the corporation's social function make pillagers of the raiders?

In these carefully reasoned dialogues, Edmund Kelly examines the impact of corporate raids on the business community and society. Kelly believes the ideal corporation translates capital and human energy into a community service institution that is ultimately greater than the sum of its parts. He knows that there are no perfect examples of the ideal, but argues convincingly that corporations left to their own devices come closer to perfection than they do when forced to combat raiding profiteers. Moreover, he hints that the future of capitalist society may depend largely on how well it protects its keystone institution, the corporation, from the destructive forces of the raiders.

Naturally, Kelly's conclusions are not well received among raiders, investment bankers, takeover lawyers, and other members of what Kelly calls the "takeover crowd." Kelly has few kind words for any of those critics. He paints a picture of investment bankers and takeover lawyers whose self-interest may have overshadowed their professional judgment.

Few people are as well qualified to raise these issues as Edmund Kelly. In November, 1967, as a young lawyer with a large Wall Street law firm, Kelly co-authored an article in The Business Lawyer that is the seminal legal treatise on takeover defenses. This, just as the earliest hostile takeovers were being explored in corporate board rooms and investment banking houses. Most takeover defenses touted today by the nation's best known takeover defense lawyers are outlined in that article, including the unusual Pac Man defense where the target attacks the raider. In 1975, then a partner in his law firm, Kelly created the first "fair price clause" for a corporate client. The "poison pill" is a version of the "fair price clause". (Kelly argues that poison pills don't work.)

Kelly played a critical role in several major takeovers, including two now-legendary fights. He was an advisor to B.F. Goodrich in its defeat of an unwanted offer from Northwest Industries and he represented the successful white knight McDermott Incorporated in saving Babcock & Wilcox from United Technologies. However, he retained a skeptical view of the utility of most defense tactics in the heat of a cash tender offer. Ultimately he refused to play the role of takeover lawyer. Twice Kelly turned down lucrative offers to serve as principal takeover counsel to leading Wall Street investment bankers. "The first hostile takeover I advised on (for the defense) was repugnant to me," he said, "I knew then as surely as I know now that it was wrong."

Instead, Kelly, now vice chairman of Dominick & Dominick, has waged a low-profile, personal war against the takeover business. There are now 19 states with fair price-type statutes based on Kelly's original concept. Kelly conceived the 1969 tax amendment (Section 279) that disallowed the deduction for all but the first $5 million of interest on convertible "funny money," and the 1984 disallowance of the dividend received credit on stock purchased by a corporation with borrowings. He has been strongly supporting a proposal that would extend Section 279 to disallow tax deductions for all but the first $5 million of interest on any kind of debt incurred to acquire another corporation's stock.

This book raises important questions of public policy about issues affecting the institutions upon which we all depend for our continued prosperity. It is important reading for anyone concerned about the future of corporate business in a capitalistic society.

--Tim Pryor

ACKNOWLEDGMENTS

The author is grateful for the advice and the constructive criticism of Paul L. Kennedy, and the encouragement of the author's family. It is hoped that the investigations presented here will be received with patient understanding, and that certain conclusions from a study of this subject over two decades will be evaluated not so much with a view to rebuttal, as in the spirit of discovering even more competent answers to these difficult questions that are so vital to us all.

PREFACE

In 1985 an editor of <u>The Wall Street Journal</u> told the author that Ivan F. Boesky, an arbitrageur, had said to the <u>Journal</u> that he would debate anyone on the subject of hostile takeovers. The editor of the <u>Journal</u> asked if the author would debate Mr. Boesky, with excerpts from the transcript to be published in the <u>Journal</u>. Although a private person, the author accepted, and it was understood the debate would be held soon at the <u>Journal's</u> offices. A few days later the editor called the author and said that Mr. Boesky would not debate him.

According to a book he wrote, Mr. Boesky's most memorable takeover contest, one in which he made a large profit and received his first national publicity, was J. Ray McDermott's acquisition of Babcock & Wilcox following a complex struggle with initial bidder United Technologies. The author was the legal strategist for McDermott.

The following dialogues are a fictionalized account and nothing in them is intended to represent the views of Mr. Boesky or necessarily of any other person, including the author.

E.J.K.

September 1987

THE FIRST DAY

Michael: Let's begin. My objection to hostile takeovers is that the established, widely held public company is an important unit of society. It has independence, self-responsibility, and with that everything about it is different than in the privately owned enterprise. It's primary objective is its own preservation and growth for the benefit of society, including shareholders. But not exclusively the shareholders. It will have blemishes from time to time but it is something quite precious, and capable of enormous good if we treat it properly. It is really a cultural event in the current development of civilization, I believe, and as such it deserves our respect. Hostile takeovers reduce the public company to a thing and exterminate it. And that's wrong. We will get from the public company what we put into it, and if we treat it like a thing it will start to act like one.

Lawrence: And that's all sentimental nonsense. I thought we were here to talk about takeovers. You're talking about mysticism. Don't forget you are dealing with business corporations here, not churches or museums or landmarks. They have owners -- the public shareholders --just as private companies do. Management of a public company ought to have one allegiance above all others -- maximizing the wealth of the shareholders. Hostile takeovers do that, and entrenched management opposition to them is an outrage. It is unpardonable. It contradicts everthing a business corporation stands for. These hired managers -- they aren't the owners of it. They're fiduciaries. Some would call them glorified floor sweepers. The spectacle of them standing in the way of a takeover is . . . it's criminal.

1

Michael: What would you have management do if they receive an uninvited takeover? Accept it?

Lawrence: No, of course not. They should negotiate. Maybe they can get more from the bidder, or from some other company. Once someone has put the company in play, they should get the best deal for the holders. That goal should shape their every strategy.

Michael: What if they think the best deal for the genuine investor holders, as well as for the company and society, is to keep the company independent and grow it in its own tradition? What if they think no one will pay today the equivalent of what they believe the company will be worth in the future as an institution?

Lawrence: Everything has a present fair value. No exceptions. That bunk about management's belief in future value is the refuge of scoundrels. On that basis, no public companies would ever be acquired.

Michael: You're dead wrong, and that's the first of the myths the takeover crowd — the group of entrepreneurs, investment bankers, lawyers and arbitrageurs that thrive on takeovers — help perpetuate. Nine out of every ten mergers of public companies are friendly negotiated deals, ones where the acquired company management initiated or cooperated with the transaction because they believed it was best. More than nine out of ten. You and your pals ignore those statistics when you go around speaking of entrenched American management. Why, Congress has even had to forbid certain friendly

2

mergers through the antitrust laws, to keep managements from arranging them. We would have more mergers if we didn't have hostile takeovers. Many deals are never put together these days because the managements involved on both sides are concerned that some raider, egged on by an investment banker, will try to break it up with a higher bid, like Texaco did to Pennzoil's merger with Getty.

Lawrence: So what's wrong with that? If you're going to sell, sell to the highest bidder. Who cares, as long as the price is high enough? There's no difference between friendly and unfriendly in the business world.

Michael: We will always have far more friendly deals than hostile ones, despite this risk of finding a strange bedfellow, and I'm surprised arbitrageurs don't recognize that. If there were no hostile deals, they could make more money working an increased number of friendly deals, mergers and leveraged buyouts.

Lawrence: Then what's so great about your precious public companies, if they agree to become privately owned again, voluntarily?

Michael: Slow down. First you indict all management for being entrenched. When I show they are not, you slip away and attack my idea of a public company. Stick to your point. The fact is managements are not overly interested in their own entrenchment. Far from it. The merger record proves that beyond any doubt. Also, the lot of the large public company manager is different and harder than it was in the days of private ownership. Much harder.

Lawrence: Why?

Michael: Precisely because there are no owners to talk with, to get approval from, to get support, reinforcement from. The owners are dispersed so far and wide as to be nonexistent for this purpose. Instead of owners now, the larger public companies have to reckon with shadowy middlemen, people who don't own the shares but who can decide to sell them in the blink of an eye. These middlemen -- you'd call them "the funds" -- are hired and fired according to whether the stock price goes up or down. You know very well, from the authoritative studies, that a company's stock price has surprisingly little to do with how that company and its management are performing. Industry and general economic factors by and large are a much bigger influence. These so-called institutional shareholders have a short horizon. Their goal is to avoid being 5th of 5 in performance every year, so a year to them is a career. They want quarter after quarter after quarter of steadily improving results in both earnings and market price. If you told them you intended to show depressed or even negative results for a year or two in order to achieve long range benefits for the company, they'd probably say "good luck" and sell the stock. After all, they can always come back when you are out of the woods again.

Now, contrast that with private companies. There the small group of owners would be the ones encouraging long range planning. Why, they'd probably fire executives who foolishly tried to live quarter to quarter. It's irresponsible. It's the antithesis of what sound business is about. I could go on with these contrasts between public and private ownership all day. So could you, and you know it.

You have it all backwards. Private ownership offers comforts to responsible managements -- not anxiety.

Lawrence: I think this long range -- short range theory is a make weight. It sounds plausible, and because it is impossible for anyone to assemble enough facts to disprove it, you management apologists all use it. You over-use it. Every time I pick up a paper or a business periodical I see some guy whining about being forced to focus on short term goals. That same guy's bonus is probably keyed to short term results. Targets of takeovers have not been known for their commitment to research. And you can't tell me that the companies whose stocks do perform well are all skimping on long range planning and investment. I'll wager they pay even more attention to long range matters and research and development than any of your laggards do. That's the very reason they do perform well over time.

Michael: I agree, but you miss my point. I did not use long range vs. short range as an argument against takeovers, at least not yet, but that day could come. You asked me why I said it is harder to be a manager in a widely held public company than in a private one. I'm telling you. The extra burden on managers who have to take currently unattractive measures, from a strictly financial or cash standpoint, is a part of the special anxiety that goes with being a responsible CEO of a public company. It's a demanding job, and vitally important to society. An enormous share of the responsibility for how this country lives and will live in the future lies in the hands of its public company executives. You better face that. They have now become the principal escorts of the capitalist process, that underpins everything. They understand it and they care for it deeply. They also know their companies, intimately. They have that sense of the reality of the enterprise, and responsibility for it, that is critical to efficient management. If we want a system that continually harasses these key people, derides them, diminishes their contribution to society, seeks new ways to discipline them for made-up failings, one day we'll have nothing left but stooge executives who live up perfectly to these degrading caricatures you draw. That, my friend, would be a terrible development. American management deserves great credit that so far they seem to have overcome the unfair insult that the takeover wave represents, and have kept their minds on the country's business. You'd have the public believe these executives are all on the golf course thinking of their next perquisites and never in the office like you are, counting your money.

Lawrence: You aren't going to get me to shed any tears for CEOs. If an entrepreneur makes money on the takeover, that's simply the proof of the pudding -- that the CEOs could have made the same money for their shareholders, but didn't. I think that all in all they are an overpaid, underworked, arrogant lot who take out much more than they give back to society. If we didn't ride herd on them, keep tightening up the SEC disclosure rules on things like personal use of corporate assets, and compensation schemes, a lot of them would run off with the store. As a group,

6

I have little respect for those people.

Michael: Now we are getting to the inside of the onion, aren't we? You favor takeovers for two reasons. On a theoretical plane, you are anti-big business. It's not really theory, you detest businessmen who head our large companies. More important, you make a lot of money from takeovers. You dress your hostility and your profiting up in all these altruistic notions about helping shareholders by making managements accountable. You don't care about average shareholders. You aren't some monk or some Peace Corps volunteer. You are a fellow that is making a fabulous fortune from takeovers. All these fancy reformist notions are uttered for one reason: It attracts more attention to you, makes you a folk hero, and that gives you more clout the next time you jump on a big company. It increases the chance they will take you seriously and run to a white knight or else buy your shares at a big profit because you are now the notorious raider and all that. You can pick any company you want and create instant wealth for yourself. But you couldn't do what you do, all your teeing companies up and your greenmailing, without the assist of your sympathetic media attention. So you court it by pretending you are helping the little guy while you are making all that money for yourself. I sometimes wonder how you can face yourself. You know that it's misleading the public, this do-gooder, Robin Hood image you cultivate.

What you cororate control entrepreneurs do is so lacking in talent or imagination, it's surprising more businessmen have not turned away from real work and taken up the same pursuit.

You get a pool of cash together from your associates and you go into the market and buy a lot of stock of a company that has a sound balance sheet, a relatively low market price compared to its earnings, and no controlling shareholder. You buy as quietly as you can, trying not to disturb the price too much as you accumulate.

Lawrence: Why are you wasting my time telling me what I do? I know what I do.

Michael: When your holdings reach 5% of the shares you announce your presence in a news release and make a brief SEC filing. Then the fur starts to fly. Inevitably the stock price goes higher merely because of your public announcement, as people anticipate a struggle for control. So right off you have made yourself a very substantial paper profit over your average cost for the shares. And so far you haven't done anything. Because the target is well run, you haven't risked anything very considerable either. Like the infamous bull pools of the 1920's you are now in a position to sell your shares into this market that you excited. If you act swiftly you can even unload before you have to amend your SEC statement to report that your holdings have dropped back below 5%. But that's the least of your options. Especially if you have enjoyed a raider reputation in the press, the management of the company you picked is understandably up in arms. So a more profitable option for you is to sell the shares back to the company at a price higher than the market.

Lawrence: I don't do things like that.

Michael: You all do it, but you try to cover it up. Most managements are willing to purchase your shares, within wide limits, because of the threat your block represents to the company's independence. Companies will pay up to 30% above the market. Your most lucrative option of all, however, is to stir up a bidding contest for control of the company. If you can prod the management into letting its eager investment bankers find a "white knight" to rescue it by acquiring it, you will make a profit far greater than if the company were to buy back your shares. You might get 30% to 50% above the market. And market now is a lot higher than cost. The investment bankers are your witting allies in all of this. Their huge fees are your single best assurance that there will be a deal if you can keep the pot boiling long enough for them to get control of the company's directors -- with or without the chief executive's support. This need for prodding management could even go so far as your having to make an offer for the whole company yourself, subject to your finding financing and similar nonsense. But that would be just for effect. The last thing you and your associates want is to own a big company. Your whole strategy is to corner the management and leave them no choice but to find another company willing to acquire the target to prevent you from acquiring it. When this white knight finally shows up, you and the other speculators make handsome portfolio profits and the low risk and low everything game moves on to the next town. And, that's what a corporate control entrepreneur does for a living.

Lawrence: You weaken your position accusing me of hypocrisy, or attacking my occupation. You display a typical businessman's loathing for the corporate control entrepreneurs. The fact of the matter is that takeovers show that there are values in companies that should be reaped by shareholders, but are not until the companies are taken over. The earnings potential of their assets, resources and market position are not being realized.

Michael: Let the alienated intellectuals, and the economists with their heads in the eighteenth century make those reform arguments of yours. Those platitudes don't lie in your mouth. Not when you're making all that money.

Lawrence: Shareholders benefit handsomely from hostile takeovers. You can't deny that. As the President's Council of Economic Advisors has said, it's proven. What's more, the economy benefits because assets are taken away from one set of managers and given to a different set of managers who can put them to better, higher uses. You can't deny that either. These two are the chief benefits of hostile takeovers. That economist The Wall Street Journal loves to quote . . .

Michael: Joseph Schumpeter.

Lawrence: . . . called it "creative destruction". This is nature's way, and it's a good way. You just want status quo, equilibrium. That's not the way the world is, or should be.

Michael: I dispute both your points. First, when you net everything out shareholders do not make money from hostile takeovers if you mean individual shareholders at large. I assume that's

10

what you mean, with all your populist talk. Not big institutions, and not arbitrageurs. Sure, every once in a long while an individual shareholder happens to own stock in a Gulf Oil or an Allied Stores and they get a windfall. But look how few large company takeovers there are in any one year. How many shareholders, and again I mean individual investors, are fortunate to own stock in more than one of the half-dozen or so large companies targeted? The arbitrageurs always benefit because they are glued to a quote machine and have their other sources. The raider always benefits, naturally. And some, but not all, of the big institutions may benefit simply because they hold so much stock or play the arbitrage game. But you exaggerate when you say shareholders generally benefit. For them it is not unlike winning a lottery. The takeover crowd makes a disproportionate share of the money from takeovers. Yet how they love to put on the sheep's clothing and say takeovers are good for the sheep!

The real problem with takeovers is that in return for a slim chance of being in on a takeover windfall, ordinary shareholders are required to invest, and, worse, the rest of society is required to exist, in an increasingly unstable environment where all managements must continually operate in the negative shadow of these takeovers. There is no hostile takeover that affects the target alone. For every one company taken over in any year, there are hundreds of public companies that have to be distracted by them. Distracted from such things as improving productivity, pursuing the latest technology, rebuilding our industrial capacity.

Instead, they spend time and money on takeover lawyers figuring out weird prophylactic measures. Always thinking of the stock market impact of whatever they plan to do -- what the funds and the analysts will think. Compelled to cash management and pure financial growth. Yet hesitating to put extra cash on the balance sheet because the company will look more attractive to a raider. Perhaps unwisely buying other companies to absorb excess cash flow that could otherwise attract raiders. Maybe taking on new debt to buy in public shares, or "restructuring" as the Wall Street crowd likes to call it. Giving up a profitable and promising line of business because temporarily the market is not reflecting the price a raider could get for it if he sold it to pay down his debts. Don't you see that all the public companies have to live this excessively market price conscious way, just because of a handful of takeovers that will actually be made each year? It's the problem of the few and the many.

You can't maintain that investor shareholders generally benefit from that nonsense. And don't say the answer is we need more takeovers. That won't happen. The number of people who will practice this craft is, fortunately, quite limited.

Lawrence: The answer is that managements should not act like you describe. You mustn't attack takeovers on the basis of these wrong-headed management responses to them. Why should a management's ability to concentrate on business be affected by the threat of a takeover?

Michael: A chief executive officer who is unfazed about the possibility of a hostile takeover would be a poor CEO, perhaps even a venal one. Any chief executive worth his title will resist the idea with all his energy, unless the price offered is remarkably high. That's what makes him good --pride in his company and its mission as an independent unit. That's the main thing that motivates him. And he certainly will take steps he thinks the company can afford to avert a takeover. If you think we'll ever have an economy where executives are neutral about their firms being taken over, then you have a dim outlook for us. I'm sure there are places in the world where businessmen sit around hoping someone will idle by and try to buy them out. Thank heaven that's not our system, that's not the present attitude among executives at our large publicly held companies. One of the many things wonderful about these companies in America is that they fill their officers with this genuine and constructive pride in the enterprise. It is more important to them than their compensation. We have to protect, encourage that spirit, because it is the absolute essence of what keeps business moving ahead. Which means it is one of the most important factors in our entire society.

Lawrence: You keep using the term "hostile takeover". Let's not forget that tender offers are "offers." They are voluntary. Stockholders have free choice to accept them or not. They read about the initial offer in the paper. A little later they get some forms in the mail. They get a mailing from their company stating management's position on the offer. All told they have at least 20 working days to decide what to do. They watch the papers because there may be higher bids. Ultimately they have three choices: One, tender their shares by signing and returning the form or asking their broker to do it. Two, sell their shares into the market, probably for a bit less than the offer price. Three, do nothing. Hold. The offer papers they get in the mail have to say what the bidder intends to do with the company after the offer is finished.

Michael: You left out paying taxes.

Lawrence: Of course, if you sell you pay taxes. This is a wonderful system we have here. Formerly if you owned stock that was it. Watch the stock prices. There was only one game in town. Now we have a system where these wonderful events can happen, to the benefit of all the shareholders. It's progress. Its voluntary. What could be more reasonable?

Michael: It is not voluntary. It is a gun to the individual shareholder's head. It's a mockery to call these things offers. You should read those documents you mention that are sent to shareholders in the offer. They include the most grim list of horrors one can imagine that await anyone who is considering not tendering, not paying taxes. They warn that the raider will eliminate the company's dividend. That the shares may also be ineligible for listing in the over-the-counter quotes, in which case price quotes won't be available in the newspapers. That the company may be deregistered by the SEC, if it has fewer than 300 shareholders left, in which case there is no assurance that financial information will be publicly available at all about its business and its condition. That the shares may not be eligible collateral for margin loans any more. And that the bidder may well decide, once it has purchased a majority of the stock, to

14

put through a merger transaction, a legal step, that will force the remaining shareholders to take even less cash than the present offer price. All of this for shareholders who yesterday thought they owned stock in a large public corporation, whose shares were widely held and actively traded on a national stock exchange.

Lawrence: There is a premium over the market price before the offer that is being paid to the shareholder. And many companies are fungible. There are a dozen oil companies that look like and perform like a Gulf or Unocal, for example. So the individual is not without choices that are essentially equivalent. If he gets a 60% premium over market for one, he can take it and buy stock in another at a 60% discount.

Michael: But that's just it, Lawrence. Some individual investors, strike that, I'll say most of them, prefer this particular company — not a company of this kind. They have an appreciation of the public company as a unique entity that you are blind to. There's also taxes. At one time when the SEC was going after one type of tender offer — where insiders of the public company seek to take it private through a tender offer — the Commission likened a tender offer to condemnation in real estate. They should have applied that same thinking to all of these offers for large public companies. You can't refuse these offers.

There are some public companies where you know up front when you invest that only 20% or 30% of the shares are traded. The rest is owned by one person. There you go in with your eyes open. That dominant shareholder controls the situation and you can be made to cash out whenever he desires, for no more than the book value, maybe less. But that's not what serious investors expect when they buy into a large widely held company, a well known company that has no controlling shareholders. They expect it will continue, unless its directors decide to recommend that it merge with some other firm.

Lawrence: This change in expectations is the price shareholders pay for the benefits of surprise takeovers. I don't feel sorry for them. They can cry all the way to the bank.

Michael: But I'm saying that many individual shareholders preferred to remain shareholders in the original public company. I suppose you would condone a system in America where people can come up and offer you a premium over what your home is worth and then say "look you have to take it. Get out."

Lawrence: That analogy is so silly I won't respond to it.

Michael: I once worked on a matter for a prominent company, a household name, where the board of directors reluctantly decided to endorse a hostile tender offer by a large foreign company when the bidder raised the initial price. A few days later I had a call from a gentleman who owned about 4% of the target company's stock. He was the largest shareholder. He said he thought tendering at this premium price was a terrible thing to have to do. His cost basis for tax purposes was just about zero. He had the highest aspirations for the company, even though recent earnings had not been good. He said he called several brokers that he trusted and they all told him he had no choice. It was a cash offer for all the shares. He had to sell. He could not afford to run the risk of being left a minority holder in a company with all the horrible consequences I just mentioned. He was wondering if I could give him any different advice. Any hope. I couldn't.

There's your voluntary tender offer.

Lawrence: To go back to your absurd example, they have a clear choice of accepting a 50% premium over the market value of their house, or not. They can remain in the house, or move on to a bigger one with the cash bonanza they get.

Michael: They can't remain. The block has changed. It's block busting. They have to accept the premium, like it or not.

Lawrence: Moving into a more expensive house with the cash windfall is not exactly an imposition. A few mavericks who don't want a cash windfall can't hold up the show for everyone else.

Michael: The problem is most individual shareholders would fall into your maverick category. But they aren't in touch with one another, and even if they were, the institutional holders will have a majority of the shares in most of our largest companies. The institutions get the papers ready to tender about ten seconds after the news of the offer hits the "broad tape". Their only questions are whether there will be a higher bid, and where to spend the proceeds.

Lawrence: This pressure on small holders is ephemeral. The SEC has stepped in to alleviate pressure, by lengthening the time offers stay open. The only "pressure" is economic choice. It's got to be that way.

Michael: No it doesn't. There is an effective "fair price" clause that several dozen companies have put in their charters since 1975 after getting shareholder approval. And eighteen states have adopted weaker versions of it into the state incorporation law. North Carolina was the first state to adopt the original strong version of it. The original fair price clause gives the shareholder a chance at getting a premium if he is forced out later in a merger, unless directors decide to waive it. He might get even more money than those who tendered initially, maybe a lot more. It turns the tables in this situation. If he chooses to continue, the shareholder will still be a first class citizen even though the company is no longer widely held. He can't be stampeded.

Lawrence: Those clauses just discourage takeovers to begin with, and therefore they enable managements to become fat and happy. Also, individual shareholders do like takeovers — so many of them now invest in takeover stocks, that it's obvious they are looking for quick profits just like anyone else. If they aren't looking for profits, they wouldn't be in the stock market to begin with. You make it sound like individual shareholders are all the kind that kept savings in passbook accounts the past five years. I don't think so.

Michael: Talk to a proxy solicitation expert if you doubt my belief about individual shareholder loyalty.

Lawrence: You started to say you disputed that takeovers bring in more capable managers who put assets to higher uses.

Michael: It's another meaningless catch-phrase, one the economists love. It's the dumbo theory. I've followed this area closely for a longer period of time than anyone. I haven't seen evidence for the superior managers and "higher uses" theory. On the contrary, the failure of General Electric's legendary management to make a success of Utah International raises profound doubts about the higher uses theory when it comes to combining large public companies. And that was a negotiated merger, which means it should have had a better chance. The people who make hostile takeovers wouldn't have made the final cuts at General Electric. They are not creative, productive entrepreneurs, let alone outstanding managers. They aren't going to manufacture Schumpeter's new consumers' goods, they aren't going to give us his new technology, new methods of production or transportation, new markets, new forms of industrial organization.

There was a time when ego alone seemed to fuel the occasional hostile takeover. Lately the bidders are usually not even operating companies. They are financially oriented special purpose entities. The name entrepreneur doesn't fit them. They are arbitrageurs at heart who go under the name "financiers." They don't have an interest in owning anything but stock, and stock is to trade. Schumpeter wouldn't have called what these people do "creative destruction". He'd have called it so many sources of social waste. If they do acquire a company in almost all cases their pattern is to load the acquired public company up with much more debt than the former directors believed would be prudent when it was independent. The U.S. taxpayer pays for this, because the raider deducts the interest expense from the target's income and to that extent the corporate income tax is reduced. Look at any of the major hostile takeovers proposed in the last few years. Get out the raider's "pro forma" statement of the target's income, the income statement that is adjusted to give effect to his deal. You'll see that only two things change. The interest expense goes up. The tax expense goes down — by a hefty proportion of what the added interest expense is. Only when Congress awakens to this situation, and disallows the interest deduction on loans incurred to make hostile stock purchases of public companies, will we have a fair test of your fancy theory about "higher uses." Right now the takeover equation reduces to: I can get more than the market price for those same assets because I'm willing to borrow against them more than you are, and the U.S. tax law still encourages me to do it with the deduction for corporate interest expense. There's your "higher uses." Taxes have been the mother's milk of the hostile takeovers. If the interest deduction were repealed, you wouldn't see as many of them.

Wilbur Mills introduced a bill that did this for interest on convertible acquisition debt back in 1969. It's an unmentionable among the tight knit takeover crowd. As you know, since that became law a raider can only deduct up to $5 million a year of interest on debt securities used as consideration in a takeover which are freely tradeable and convertible into common stock. It was the only example ever of the tax code disallowing an interest expense of a public corporation. At the time, Northwest Industries' $690 million offer of convertible securities for B.F. Goodrich was the largest non-governmental debt offering in U.S. history to that date. Mills foresaw that the Treasury would be subsidizing a wave of corporate takeovers unless this limitation was imposed. The raiders would take advantage of the liquidity in our secondary markets in stocks, tie their "chinese paper" or "funny money" to that liquidity with the convertible feature, and then use these hybrid debt securities in lieu of cash to make their takeovers. Print the stuff in their basements. When Mills acted he set back the takeover movement 15 years. It wasn't until the major clients that do business as Drexel Burnham came up with a fall back plan — a way to achieve a semblance of liquidity for straight junk bonds not tied to the equity markets — that the takeovers were able to stage a breakout, starting with the hostile Unocal bid by Pickens in late 1984. As you know, traditionally the corporate bond secondary markets in the U.S. have been relatively illiquid. The dollar amount of corporate bonds traded on a secondary basis is slight compared to the vast dollar amount of stocks. Many corporate bonds seldom trade at all. The dollar amount of corporate bonds traded in a day on the New York Stock Exchange is paltry. Drexel Burnham's network of clients acted as though they have solved this, and thereby made junk debt a usable medium of takeover exchange -- or at least financing. It's still not clear that a real secondary market has been made. But people have been persuaded that it is there, and perception is the bulk of the challenge.

Lawrence: Spare me the lecture about how the bond markets work, O.K.? I've forgotten more about that than you'll ever know.

Michael: I'm sure you have, I'm sure you have. And the fellows out there with good ideas for new products, new services, don't know anything about the bond markets. And probably never will.

Lawrence: But you have conceded that the financiers know how to make more money with the same assets. All I am saying is that managements, with a fiduciary duty to shareholders, ought to be making the same money for the shareholders. It's really the same thing that goes on in leveraged buyouts. Do you object to leveraged buyouts?

Michael: Not at all. They serve a good purpose in our economy. When owners of private companies, or managers of public companies, decide that the company or a division of it should be sold, we must have a mechanism for allocating capital to potential buyers. That's healthy and it's essential. But the leveraged buyouts have by and large been negotiated deals. That's the key. What the raiders are groping for today is leveraged <u>hostile</u> buyouts. I can't find any good in that at all.

Lawrence: Your distinction is flimsy. If LBOs are okay, then you agree a high level of debt is okay. Why does it matter whether management goes along or is dragged along? Who cares. A sale is a sale. Debt is debt. It's all the same to the shareholders who reap the profits.

Michael: You are bringing us back to the bedrock issue in all this -- the stature of a public company. The longer it has been publicly held, the greater its stature. I see grave danger in treating these entities like they were things. There is a great deal at stake here. You have no idea what I'm talking about.

Lawrence: I sure don't. Look. We could take a large division of XYZ Corporation tomorrow and take it public. Either sell all its shares to the public through underwriters, or spin the shares off to XYZ's existing shareholders. There. It's done. It's public. Now, what's changed? It now deserves more respect? Come off it.

Michael: A newly spun off company is neither fish nor fowl. If you ever studied one closely you'd know that they go through a difficult period of adjustment -- just like a company that has had its first public offering. No, I'm not talking about those exactly and you shouldn't use that example to belittle my point. I'm talking about our large public companies that have been public for decades now. Enormous, complex enterprises that have done things for us that private companies could not possibly have done. These are the precious national resources I'm concerned about. These companies have adapted fully to the separation of management from share ownership and they are working as well as ever, better. That's a marvelous thing, confounding all the economic prophets. In substitution, they have developed their individual traditions, some passing to a third or fourth generation. All in all they have behaved well and made untold contributions to society. They have literally raised the standard of life of the general population. These companies must be preserved. Our entire economic order is dependent on them. They are capable of extraordinary good for society, including shareholders, but including many others in society besides shareholders. Too many people depend upon these large companies now. We must never forget that when we are thinking of stock prices and the limited interests of present shareholders.

The public companies also represent a diversity of opinion and of method among the corporate community. That too is critically important. Their multiplicity appeals to a sound instinct that runs deep in America, a sense that when it comes to economic power centers more is better, the concern about too much decision making, too much power in too few hands. Go back some time and study the history of the U.S. banking laws if you want a good example of how we as a people have always favored keeping the wealth, the capital spread out as much as efficiently possible. Even at the risk of financial calamity, which is what we got in the 1930s. I suppose I'm getting off the subject. . .

Lawrence: What's new?

Michael: . . . but not really, because the broader implications of this takeover activity are quite omnious.

I'll be the first to confess that my idea of the uniqueness, the increasingly critical role of the public company is not fully formed. But I speak out on it because unless something is done to curb the takeovers, this headlong rush to liquidity, we will not have the independent public companies with us when we come to appreciate the scale of their changing significance. I don't mean just the managements. I don't mean just the workers. I don't mean the communities, or the suppliers, or the customers. Although they are all important and deserving of consideration in the discussion of takeovers. I mean the autonomous public companies themselves. The institutions, they're what's priceless. They embody all the others, but so much more. As certain cultural foundation stones of capitalism have weakened and worn away, the role of the public companies has assumed new meaning.

Lawrence: Your debating strategy is to widen the issues out to embrace such amorphous concepts that it becomes philosophy rather than investing.

Michael: This is a philosophical question. Tell me, Lawrence, were you reared in a setting that respected large businesses?

Lawrence: Hardly. Business has been responsible for much cruel injustice in this country. You know that, don't you?

Michael: Yes. But so much more good. Most people are not in any position to appreciate the complex good in the activity of large public business corporations. Too few come from an environment that could bring out the genuine worth in such companies, although that is changing slowly. And historically businessmen have been scorned, unable to explain their dreary, unemotional calling to the public. At best it's boring, all those figures. This is too bad, but it is also maybe the nature of business' lot —I mean, not to be understood. Even an object of hostility.

It's like expecting anything deep and fundamental to stand up and defend its significance in the grand motion of things. Usually, the most important facts are the ones privileged to go unrecognized. It is up to our elected political representatives, therefore, to see clearly how significant public companies are to all of us, and to challenge the popular myths and build consensus among the citizenry in support of those conditions the large business corporations must have to function freely. Our more responsible politicians in Washington must eventually see the harm in these hostile takeovers. They must have the courage to speak out even though it may seem unpopular to do so. This has already happened in the states, perhaps because they are closer to it, and also because the growing corporate influence in America may create less tension there.

Business will always need the thoughtful protection of society's leadership, the professional politician. It is incapable of itself supplying the leadership or the protection.

Lawrence: Let's come home to basics. A corporation is an association of shareowners -- capitalists — who band together in business and get a charter, a certificate of incorporation, from one of the states that limits their personal legal liability for any debts the business incurs. That's the purpose of it.

Michael: That's the result of it.

Lawrence: The purpose is not to create some new "person" that will then go tooting off on its own and do whatever it pleases. The shareowners own the business. The stock certificate is like a deed that represents the capital they put in. The company doesn't own itself.

Michael: Right. And the shareholders are responsible for seeing to the day to day management of the enterprise. Either they must manage it personally or they must personally select the manager and supervise him.

Lawrence: Okay, then eventually the original shares get divided up and bequeathed or sold or whatever to a lot more people than the original group. Or the corporation is caused by the owner-managers to sell additional shares to the public to raise cash. Or else it issues new shares in an acquisition of some other companies that already have lots of shareholders. Now it is a "public" company, over 500 shareholders, say. Eventually there is no person or affiliated group of persons that own more than 5% of the stock. You . . .

Michael: Now it's different. Maybe it was not intended to be different when we developed incorporation laws, and let people disassociate themselves, sell their corporate shares to others as tokens of an interest in the corporate property. The English lawyers and merchants who experienced the possibly spontaneous appearance of the corporation idea probably never dreamed of today's giant public companies. Adam Smith didn't think the corporate form of business would work at all. How often the better things happen despite us. Once the public company grew in size, inversely as the concentration of ownership, it started to change. For the better. Eventually it became an elegant and exciting new medium for social as well as economic progress. All of the precepts that applied to it as a privately owned corporation now had to be reexamined, to see if they were still suitable. We are just at the earliest stages of that reexamination. We have a lot of thinking and analyzing ahead of us. Among other professionals this task will require competent, wise and courageous judges, persons specially versed in the origin and development and importance of the widely held corporation. For example, if a court is asked to rule on the extraordinarily wide powers of publicly elected directors during their term of office, it would be most unsatisfactory to rely for precedent on a court case decided at the earliest stages in the rapid evolution of the modern public company. And the states will surely have to adapt their public company corporation statutes in the decades ahead. The public company is far ahead of us all. We must strive to catch up with it and accomodate our system to it.

You plain and simply distrust public companies, I mean their executives, don't you?

Lawrence: I do, most of them, and they earned it. What was it that President Kennedy's father told him about businessmen?

Michael: I'm afraid President Kennedy's father had the same attitude you do. In fact, in his hey day on Wall Street he might have done some things like the things you do, the 1920s version of putting stocks "in play."

28

Lawrence: Look at the foreign payments scandals, the commercial bribery. How about Equity Funding, and the other cases of securities fraud? What about the epidemic of corporate slush funds we uncovered not too long ago? And the accounting irregularities by large public companies. Look at the recent cases where courts are prosecuting executives for manslaughter as a result of defective products, or plant safety failures. Need I go on? At one time people were urging the Justice Department to establish a Division of Corporate Crime.

Michael: That was Ralph Nader. There was no public consensus for that.

Lawrence: You know you can't defend big business across the board. It's like carrying water in a sieve. The wrongdoing, the greed has been too well documented.

Michael: In your list, you are mixing two kinds of wrongs indiscriminately — the ones where the businessman lined his own pockets and the ones where what he did, though wrong, he did for the company's benefit. I'm not saying there have been no abuses, no wrongdoers, but I do defend public companies absolutely and public company managements generally. I would probably be more ruthless with the wrongdoers in public companies, the cheats, than you would. But you cannot use periodic management wrongdoing to justify blanket condemnation of what to me is one of the most important groups in our society. Let alone to justify ending a public company's existence.

Lawrence: You're not seriously putting

public company executives in a class with motherhood.

Michael: To my mind, aside from direct responsibility for moulding the individual and one's human values, the most important function in society is that of deciding how the aggregate of financial and human resources will be saved and used for the satisfaction of wants. Under our form of government, which is shaped intimately by our form of enterprise, the people who have the primary responsibility for that are the senior executives of our large business corporations, most of which are publicly held. Generally, these people do a commendable job and have throughout your whole lifetime. If they face problems now, they've faced them well before. I don't regard them as overcompensated and I certainly don't regard them as smug or incompetent or entrenched. It is the fact that the managements are not directly responsible to owners — that ultimately the board of directors more or less perpetuates itself and the structure beneath it as critics charge -- that has much to do with the astounding and accelerating growth and success of these companies over the past three quarters of a century. No owner with real clout is anywhere in sight. Yet these entities may have behaved and performed far better than if owners had been there in person. Think of that. They are part of a new, and I think much higher process, yet still centered in the capitalist tradition. As I said, it will take much additional examination and synthesis before we can explain what it is about the modern public company that makes it such a powerful new influence. And where it is taking us. I'm not clear on it myself yet. But I assure you it is special.

Lawrence: Maybe public companies behaved well for the first half of this century because executives still believed they were answerable to someone, the shareholders, the directors, someone other than themselves. Maybe it started dawning on them in the late '60s that they are free to act as they please. Maybe the takeover arrived just in the nick of time.

Michael: There is no evidence for that theory. For several decades now public company management has been well aware that it in effect perpetuates itself. That circumstance has been widely noted. Management has had the opportunity to plunder the new order, but it has behaved admirably. At least until the takeovers arrived.

Any vote in favor of hostile takeovers is fundamentally a vote against this phenomenon of the responsible widely held public company. The takeovers are capable of perverting and eventually destroying all the benefit in this force while it is still nascent, as historic cultural changes are measured. In the final analysis you cannot have an independent public company economy and hostile takeovers side-by-side. It won't last. It can't.

Lawrence: Takeovers are not necessarily a vote against the public company -- just against certain ones who might do better as part of another public company, for example.

Michael: Once you combine a public company into another one it's gone. The acquiring tradition takes over completely. Unless it is the rare case where the target's own management rises swiftly to the top of the acquiror. But particular takeovers are not the main issue. The idea of takeovers, the universal threat of them. That's the problem.

Lawrence: I can see your zeal. But you're talking a language that is foreign to me. I can't get worked up about this dignity of a public company idea. To me, it is just a bunch of managers who don't have any real bosses. That law professor at Columbia — Berle — wrote about that fifty years ago. The separation of management from ownership. That's all it is.

Look at the ridiculous procedure that sustains corporate managements in office. The directors, the governing body provided for in the corporate charter, they are all individuals initially suggested by the chief executive officer or his predecessors. Shareholders are too widely dispersed to have any communication with each other about such things.

Michael: Shareholders are also coming and going in the stock market, constantly. Management is there, constantly. And few shareholders have their portfolio tied up with one stock either. They're diversified.

Lawrence: The incumbent directors call an annual meeting once a year and nominate themselves and any new ones they want for election to a new term. Shareholders who wish to vote can either come to the meeting or sign a company card appointing an agent to vote their shares for them by proxy. This agent is a person chosen by the management and obedient to them. The agent customarily gets authority in this way to vote a majority of the absentee shares at the meeting and he votes them all for the management nominees. And that's how directors are elected by shareholders each year. The first thing they do is have a directors' meeting and elect the chief executive and the other officers. And when the CEO retires they usually elect one of his buddies, a good guy, the kind you like to go drinking with. So it goes. Management uses the corporate funds to conduct this farce voting procedure. When there is a rare shareholder revolt, and insurgents solicit counter-proxies against management, the management still gets to use the corporate treasury for all of its expenses, while the outsiders must put up their own money for expenses, at least until they win.

Have you ever heard of anything so irresponsible? So banana republic? The chief executive selects the directors. They turn around and select the chief executive?

Michael: That's been going on for more than a few years.

Most references to the Berle and Means view on the separation of management and ownership are taken out of context. I don't think they had the same regard for the plenary authority of shareholders as you, nor the same contempt for unaccountable management. Berle once observed that shareholders contribute neither savings nor management to a corporation. All they do is maintain each other's liquidity in the secondary stock markets. I think Berle and Means may have been closer to my deeply respectful view of the public corporation than to your view. What we could use today are a new

Berle and Means who would analyze the separation of _voting_ from ownership. That has slipped by without as much attention. It has been building slowly since the late 1950s. In the largest corporations today, a majority of the shares are voted by these fund managers I referred to. They're liquidity specialists. They don't own any of the stock. First we had the emergence of public shareowners with no responsibility for the company. They just own the pieces of paper, and trade them. Now we have people claiming the control who don't even own the paper. They don't own anything, nor do they have responsibility for anything. It's no longer investment in the classical sense. Some of them are even talking about renting their votes to others. Can you believe it? The real owners are far removed workers, people employed by other large corporations. The stock has been purchased by the fund managers with the workers' pension funds. The real owners are probably just as concerned about takeovers as I am. It could happen to their company, and they wouldn't like that. But they have no control at all over the people that vote the stock. Lately we even have the spectacle of people in government egging the fund managers on to use their separated voting power to instigate more takeovers.

Lawrence: Votes are just one element of stock ownership. If separating votes gives more value to the shareholder-owner, that should be promoted. Also, aren't you concerned about keeping businessmen on their toes? Don't you think that's important? Come on, now, isn't there a risk they will become complacent? You know as well as I do a CEO controls his directors, and they in turn are patient with his failures. Doesn't that

34

bother you? Surely you see a need for accountability somewhere in your fantasyland. That's what the threat of a takeover does. It keeps these guys on their toes. It is the looming force that squeezes the inefficient managers out and puts in more capable ones.

Michael: There you go again with the distrust angle. You see a board as a group that doesn't do its job because the CEO has it wired. To my mind, a board of a public company is not there to ride herd on a CEO, except in the most egregious situations, and boards fulfill that role when it's necessary.

Lawrence: But they only act when the outside world forces their hand —the media or creditors.

Michael: We're talking about public companies. What do you want? A few CEOs fired for no apparent reason now and then. A "That's for nothing, now do something" atmosphere in the board room?

Lawrence: You know what I mean.

Michael: A substantial part of the board's function is observing senior managers for the purpose of selecting the next CEO. Otherwise the board is there to counsel, to support, to be a sounding board and to share responsibility if something goes wrong. And to do certain things required by statute, such as declare dividends. It's a team effort — the CEO in charge day-to-day, the board being a diverse group of experienced people with privilege standing close to -- but not running -- the corporation, so they are in a position to supplement the abilities of the executive officers, principally the CEO. That's the way it works, and the way it should work, and it has worked very well.

So I agree with you that absent extraordinary circumstances, when they must dismiss him, the board is not a proprietary check on a CEO. It shouldn't be, or else it will inevitably be an adversary, and that would confound its true purpose. The board of the modern public company is a stage in the transition from the private owner's selection and supervision of hired management.

But you are closing your eyes if you think the public company CEO has less motivation, is under less discipline than his private company counterpart. The most important incentive and deterrent hanging over a CEO of a public company is the fact that his company is public, and he has his own professional prestige and reputation to uphold. The efficacy of human self-esteem antedates Adam Smith. The theory underlying our Federal securities laws is that sunlight is the best disinfectant. People will not engage in self dealing if it has to be disclosed. That helps to protect us against wrong doing at large companies, and our courts will act where it doesn't. A similar reasoning applies with even greater force to the performance of management responsibility in the widely held public company. No self-respecting person is going to do a careless or second rate job of managing such a public company when he knows that all the grim details will be made public, certified by a national accounting firm. And then the financial press and the securities analysts will write about it. The

CEO of a poorly performing public company must face his peers in the business community with his embarassingly poor results, the market price suffers and he sees the value of stock options dwindle, he faces the scrutiny of debt rating agencies, he loses good people and incurs difficulty attracting new management personnel, he risks demoralizing the employee work force, and that feeds on itself. Professor Galbraith noted some of these conditions twenty years ago. Overlaying this, the incentive and positive discipline arising from the executive's position within groups and tiers at the large company is still little understood but probably a powerful factor. One could go on and on. You pro-takeover supporters ignore these influences, and spread the welcome notion that public company management is complacent because they are not subject to any disciplines. You talk like 18th century Scottish tradesmen. If the psychologists studied it I'm certain they would find that positive stresses on public company top executives exceed those bearing on the private company executive with similar functions, and exceed those bearing on wage earners in most walks of life. Theirs is not a happy-go-lucky existence.

Lawrence: Only dry eyes here.

Michael: I'll admit that there are other opponents of hostile takeovers, who do not see the significance and the potential of the public company as an institution, an institution which shapes its leaders. In view of diminishing shareholder influence, they feel a need to search for substitute executive accountability -- in the independent outside directors. But that won't work. While the directors play a key role, they cannot stand in for owners. Eventually it will be seen that within the wide latitude allowed by vigilant director participation in corporate affairs, it is to the institution and its own self that operating management must be primarily accountable. If that doesn't work then the independent public company doesn't work. It does work and there is history to prove it.

Lawrence: You can't really think the pre-existing incentives will be enough? That they will cause management to dis-integrate operations that should be separate, to get rid of divisions that aren't performing, shave staffs where there's fat, reallocate budget dollars to the most productive research? Those CEOs need the threat of takeovers to give them an incentive to change the business, because it often means reversing decisions they themselves made. It means cutting back their own empires. Some takeovers can be paid for just with the savings in corporate overhead.

Michael: I am confident that they will do all these things without the threat of takeovers, provided they are indeed appropriate and enduring measures. Business is not just a competing set of rates of return. Where the actions are appropriate, they may not do them on your timetable, but they will do them, because there are better incentives built into our system that encourage such measures for the good of the institution. The record of companies having done all of these things is there. If anything, the possibility of a hostile takeover was a cause for hesitation rather than a motive; worry about excess cash proceeds in transition, and the effect of write-offs on the market price. Our system does work. It is not broken. It has no need for takeovers.

Lawrence: Will they leverage the company up, though, and increase its debt-equity ratio and pay the debt proceeds to the shareholders? Return money to the capital markets.

Michael: Ah. As we might have expected all along, it turns out you are not talking about the quality of management at all. You're talking about the attitude, the temperment of management, the appetite for extraordinary risk. Here we go with probably the takeover crowd's chief myth. Any apprentice in the controller's department in a large public company can show you how to invert its debt- equity ratio. Lenders will come running, and the borrowings will produce cash which can then be used to buy out shareholders. Enhancement of shareholder values! That is what you are trying to intimidate public companies into doing involuntarily. "Your balance sheet or your life" is your highwayman's threat. It isn't managerial skill involved here at all. Far from it. It's pretty crude actually. It's what the high school kids in the souped-up cars used to call "chicken."

Lawrence: Nothing so pejorative. Managements need our goading to get the job done, for the benefit of their shareholders. Without us, they'd just sit there and let that borrowing capacity go to waste. Also the added leverage acts as a discipline on future management, which must run the company in a way that will pay the debt.

Michael: You have no shame, do you?   I

39

won't say now that your outsider's opinion as to a given company's appropriate debt level is necessarily wrong. Some thoughtful experts not part of the takeover crowd hold that American public companies generally have too little debt, that they are too conservative, and that foreign competitors are taking advantage of that self-imposed handicap in the struggle for world markets. But I will say, emphatically, that a large public company's debt level should be the voluntary, deliberate decision of its own management, made in the face of business conditions as management sees them. A public company should not be pressured from the outside by stock speculators into taking on debt levels that management believes to be unwise. Pressures to carry much greater debt may arise in the normal course from such things as calamities, from business setbacks, from taking advantage of new business startup opportunitites, of attractive acquisitions, and so on. But we cannot let greedy bands of stock market speculators, looking for a fast buck and on the whole unfamiliar with a company's business, foist these decisions on management, in my opinion. This is the prime distinction between a private company, where shareholders are always there and involved in the consequences, and a widely held public company where shareholders can leave any time, where they have liquidity which means they are not themselves responsible for any of it. As someone once said, if the horse dies they don't have to bury it. When companies became widely held by the public, shareholders yielded the right to dictate such things as the level of debt. Debt incurred by large enterprises should be a legitimate business necessity, in the judgement of management. To let bands of Wall Street marauders go from company to company blackjacking the managements into higher involuntary debt is wrong.

Lawrence: Why? What's wrong with it?

Michael: Put it this way. Why don't you stake your public case on that? Instead of all the propaganda about shareholders' rights and the accountability of incompetent management, why don't you tell the public that your primary goal is to make all the big public companies go deeper into debt and pay the proceeds to shareholders. You can sponsor a contest: which will grow faster, the Federal debt or the corporate debt? You can have rallies where people stage debt demonstrations, and give Man of the Year awards to the CEO who managed to borrow the most money. One of the many things wrong with it is that you have enough political acumen not to tell the public that this is all that the takeovers stand for. It's a bad joke on the country by a self-interested group of people.

Lawrence: Companies don't necessarily have to incur debt. There are other things they can do to enhance shareholder values and that help streamline the economy. They can sell off divisions in which investors lack confidence and use the proceeds to purchase their own stock. We make them do that. That's progress. Those cash proceeds are then invested by the public in new and more promising industries, biotechnology for example, strengthening the economy.

Michael: Here again, let's be clear. We are not talking about operating management ability at all, are we? We are talking about how to arrange a company so that it might yield the highest stock market value. Now. Today. No other mission.

Your point about recycling capital into more promising companies is a presumptous make-weight. Nobody knows where the money will go. It might go into the stock of a future takeover target, just like your money. Increasingly, the market no longer performs its classical purpose of channeling savings into businesses that use them to produce goods and services for society. This obsession with liquidity is draining money away from useful investment. We have to focus on where the money comes from, the "down sizing", as you folks put it, of large American companies, reconcentrating them on their core businesses.

Splitting up a big company entails measures that are negative from the standpoint of sound management of continuing operations. And it would certainly offer choice opportunities for greater wealth and financial security to the supposed entrenched management. They could head up the subsidized LBO vehicle that buys the division. Yet they customarily resist the disassembly idea because of their dedication to the whole company as company. I said the apprentice in the controller's department. If you want to be extreme, the head janitor could call in the auctioneers and tell them to break it all up and get the best price for the parts. It would likely exceed the market price. Sell the headquarters. Fire the general corporate staff. Terminate the pension plans, buy annuities for the participants and distribute the excess. Sell all the ingredient business units as free standing little companies. There. That's the end of that 70 year old firm. Is that what we want our large public companies to do? Disembowel themselves at any opportunity? Operate to liquidate at the first chance of beating the market price? Even assuming every company could do it, all at once, which is lunacy, is that how you would get the best out of all the people in a large organization? Why stop there? Why shouldn't the states sell off large parts of themselves, at least a couple of big cities? How about the U.S. selling Puerto Rico, or maybe the Virgin Islands? It might ease the deficit problem. And the museums, why don't we open them up and put all those slow moving treasures to higher uses? The libraries, the national parks. The universities. Let's sell everything.

Well, you know that's not possible, don't you. Keynes warned long ago that the entire community cannot have liquidity of investment. That's the vice in liquidity.

As individual shareowners and as members of society we benefitted beyond reckoning when we moved to an economy of large public corporations. We also accepted an unwritten compact, whether we were aware of it or not. Which is that we no longer have the right, shareholders no longer have the right, to manipulate those entities as if they were still closely held 19th century factories. In return for our new found liquidity and risk diversification and our freedom from any responsibility as owners, those entities have long since been affected with a higher interest. Their managements now answer to a more complex call of evolving capitalism. Too many people have observed this compact, for too long, for you to have the right to take your fist and break it.

Lawrence: Who's going to stop me?

Michael: And the consequences of this behavior as ideal are so utterly corrupting for the majority of public companies which cannot possibly participate in the occasional benefit that only knaves and fools would condone the activity in society. It appeals to the worst instinct in all of human nature, the inclination to outwit the community, no matter the general harm, and reap a quick profit for oneself.

Lawrence: The ultimate discipline on the public company CEO is the market. Someone being paid that much money should be willing to face the reality of market discipline. If he doesn't want that, he shouldn't have the job. And if he is not performing according to the market, someone who will perform should become a manager.

Michael: No. We cannot let the market be the test. We discussed that when we began. You are hopelessly out of date. A good performance by management is but a minor part of market price performance. It is corrupting to grade management primarily by market prices of stocks.

Lawrence: When a stock gets overlooked in the market, that's not accidental. It means an ever larger number of money managers don't have confidence in it.

Michael: We're talking about management. The world's premier computer company suffers earnings erosion because the price of oil has fallen sharply. Oil companies are leading purchasers of computers. That's the fault of the

44

computer firm's management? Another company announces sharply higher earnings and sees its market price remain the same, it's price/earnings multiple go down. Management control over earnings is quite limited. Management control over stock price is even more limited. It was not so many years ago that the SEC absolutely forbade companies from projecting their earnings for any future period no matter how short. I knew one veteran staffer at the Commission who told me projection of earnings would never, ever be lawful, in his opinion, because it was inherently deceptive and manipulative. The basis for the policy was, of course, management's assumed inability to control profits. It's amazing that the fiction of the takeover as incentive has gotten as far as it has today. We need a modern David Hume to expose this fallacy of causation.

Suppose I told you I would strike you with a stick every time it rained on a Monday. You can hope and pray it won't rain on Monday, and you can be distracted by worry that it will. But what are you going to do to prevent it? For sure. Nothing. What you're going to do is try to prevent me from striking you, because you know you can't stop the rain.

Lawrence: So all CEOs of public companies are doing a good job by your standards. Let's go home.

Michael: Be serious. I think most CEOs of large public companies are doing their job to the best of their ability in the circumstances. They aren't goofing off. They don't fit the image you fellows love to portray. Some are less able than others, I'll readily concede that.

Lawrence: Terrific. What do we do about them?

Michael: I'll tell you one thing we should not do about them, and that is extinguish the independence of the public company, break it up or make it a division of some other company, obliterate its status as a separate unit of society, just to correct a management problem, presently judged. That's hunting rabbits with a howitzer. I would rely on the customary punitive influences I've mentioned to correct the situation. They got us this far. The possibility of a proxy contest is also there.

Lawrence: You don't disapprove of those?

Michael: Not at our present stage of corporate development. Why should I?

Lawrence: Because you are such a staunch supporter of incumbent management. You think their attention is unduly diverted by takeovers. That impairs their performance.

Michael: Hold on. I'm a believer in the dignity of the large, widely held public corporation as a predominant new unit of society. Period. I am not a supporter of management as such. If they have performed in a way that attracts a traditional proxy fight, from others who want to run the company for the benefit of all shareholders -- not break it up -- then perhaps they need to be distracted. As I've said, I would probably deal much more harshly with venal or lazy managers than you would, because I have respect for their calling. You would eradicate the whole company to root out one incompetent CEO

46

-- at least that's your cover story. That's barbaric.

Lawrence: Isn't that a bit strong?

Michael: The Japanese and the West Germans consider uninvited takeovers to be barbaric. Maybe that's why their economies are doing better in areas like employee dedication, quality control and productivity. What's more, your arguments about improving management are wholly theoretical and diversionary. Let's take the gloves off, Lawrence. The record is that your raiders never pick on the poorly managed companies. You go after the good ones, the ones with hidden values, the ones the stock market has not appreciated. The ones that have been run so prudently that they can support incredibly high levels of takeover indebtedness without breaking under the strain. You wouldn't touch a W.T. Grant or a Penn Central or a Chrysler when it was ailing so. You people are using the battle cry of "oust entrenched management" to camouflage something else you are doing, something that has nothing to do with entrenched management. It has to do with taxes and interest, with risking and making money, and the raiders are not about to risk money on a dog. One can refute all your arguments about management selfishness and incompetency with a single point: Tell me this, what is the ultimate takeover defense, aside from being privately owned, or at least majority owned by friends?

Lawrence: I don't know what you're driving at.

Michael: You do too. But you'd rather not

47

talk about it. The ultimate takeover defense is to permit the company to run down. Let it turn into a derelict of accounting losses that can only limp from year to year, yet still supporting the executives and the workforce. That's entirely possible to do. It requires no action, only neglect. If takeovers, the threat of them, give management any incentive at all, that's the incentive. To fall back. Not to be up on one's toes all the time. Not to keep the company in a condition where it is safe for the potential raider's financial maneuvers. It may invite a proxy contest, this studied mediocrity, but it will never invite a unilateral cash takeover. I guarantee it. So you see takeovers attack optimism itself. They turn our managers away from the interests of society and toward base self interest. In tribute to American management, I haven't yet heard of a public company that has adopted this crass approach to the growing takeover threat. But I'll tell you something. You and your pals persist in playing this charade about the value of takeovers, and we will come to that one day. The rash of those grotesque "poison pill" plans is an early warning signal. We could reach a point where malicious takeover tension between self preservation and excellence becomes too much, where managers finally react to the gross inequity of the takeover as discipline and say "The heck with it, let the place fall behind so they'll leave us be." If that day ever arrives the takeover interests will have done incalculable damage to this country and its people. At its roots capitalism is a state of mind, a series of simple human motivations. You succeed in breaking the hope and the spirit of our leading American managers with your self-centered antics and no rebuke would be too harsh for you folks, in my opinion.

At every company I know of the executives are in effect working in every way to make the company a more likely takeover target. That is, they are doing their best to run it well, so that you and your ilk might have the opportunity to come along one day, taking advantage of distortions in the stock market, and make a profit by loading it up with debt or breaking it up or whatever else you can do to make a quick profit. That state of affairs will not last. It defies the gravity known as human nature.

Lawrence: I still don't see how you allow proxy contests but would ban cash takeovers. What's the difference? In both cases the incompetents are thrown out.

Michael: Your dumbo theory has just been refuted in the case of takeover targets. In the proxy contest new management takes the helm of the same public company.

In the takeover you are eliminating this precious, self-responsible entity because temporarily some will say it is performing poorly --but not so poorly as to scare off raiders. The proxy contest is intended to correct the perceived ailment without killing the patient. To bring fresh ideas to the management role. That's entirely legitimate for now.

Lawrence: What do you mean "For now"?

Michael: The public company is dynamic. There may come a day when the performance of the large public company requires even more autonomy, when it will not permit uninformed, unrealistic and unresponsible shareholder participation in selection of those who manage the complex and prolonged tasks of the enterprise. But if that happens, effective alternative disciplines of advanced group rituals within the large scale corporate organization will already have become apparent and satisfactory to most of us. That's a long ways off.

In today's proxy contest the shareholders are told, "Stay here with this company and support us, the insurgents, in making it better for everyone." That's a good thing. In the takeover bid, shareholders are told "Here, take this money and get out of here. Go invest in something else. We are going to make the company a private company again and run it exclusively for our own benefit, and you'll never know the details." There is a world of difference there.

You supporters of hostile takeovers have taken your worn-out battle cries from the proxy fights. In the proxy contest the ideas of "entrenched management," "new and better managerial skills," and so on, have their place. You folks have lifted them and transported them into the hostile takeover debate where they have no place, and indeed become a mockery.

Lawrence: All raiders do in many cases is buy stock and urge the management to increase shareholder values -- in your words, they "bring fresh ideas to management" which is "entirely legitimate." It's only when management selfishly doesn't respond that further action in aid of shareholders is taken.

50

Michael: But, again, there the threat is not to enlist the support of other holders as in a proxy fight. The threat is to cash out the other holders. And that's what distinguishes the target of a tender offer from the target of a proxy contest. The takeover target may be poorly run but it is still considered a safe enough place to invest a great amount of the raiders money.

Lawrence: Maybe we have covered enough for today. And you must be weary because you're doing most of the talking. Let's reflect on each other positions and resume this in the morning.

THE SECOND DAY

Lawrence: You have said noble things about your view of the corporate world. I think you're living a fantasy. What goes on in the conventional corporate establishment is not what you hope. Those large companies become fat and inefficient, bloated with unnecessary managerial personnel. They are dens of pointless politics, people covering their own rear ends. The CEOs are usually the ones who have been caught making the fewest mistakes. The ones who went to the right schools, have attractive wives. They have more political savvy and social graces than smarts.

Establishment industrial corporations have far too many layers of middle management, most of them supporting their own baliwicks. The whole system generates excessive paperwork and interminable unproductive meetings. The companies underinvest in research and development and stifle imagination and initiative down in the ranks. They penalize people who do dare to innovate. Most of those senior managers should be out in the plants with their hands dirty, not in the glass towers with the expensive dining rooms on the highest floor and the stretch limousines in the basement. Those top people you admire are selfish, arrogant, interested in one thing only -- their own well being, which they always identify with the corporation, when in truth they may be the worst thing happening to the corporation. If we are not always on our guard, if we do not have a club constantly over senior managers' heads, they will not perform at their peak, and the worst of them will steal the companies blind. That's the real world. That's what's hurting this country, not the takeovers. I know some of this may be in the eye of the beholder, but you are just naive.

Michael: You told me to stay out of the bond business. Why are you so comfortable in the executive suite? Where did you learn about CEOs and their wives and life in a large corporation? I grant what you say about the creeping inefficiencies, which go with large organizations and which always need attention. But not your prejudice, your scorn for the persons. The overwhelming majority of top business executives are probably decent, extremely hard working and conscientious people. They are not heroic, they certainly are not glamourous but they are the backbone of the whole economy. And it's a good economy, warts and all. The fact that the public and the arts have never admired them, like we do a cowboy or a Supreme Court justice, is neither here nor there. As I said yesterday, it's nature's way that they should labor at their ledgers and their tedious pursuits without public understanding let alone affection. But you aren't the public. You know finance, at least. Where do you get these pagan, stereotype notions of what the businessmen are like who lead large public companies?

Lawrence: Everybody knows what they are like. It's common sense. The thing that convicts them all in the public eye is the compensation, and the perquisites. Too many times we have seen the profits decline but not the CEO's salary. Too many times we've seen layoffs that devestate thousands of families, and the executives don't even take a pay cut.

Michael: You have no interest to improve business. You detest the people who run large companies, regardless of what kind of job they're doing. You and your pals use analogies to breeding dogs when you speak of them. But you have a good thing going for you there. The public has little use for business executives. You can make a personal fortune harassing business executives with takeovers. Combine the two and you're a folk hero and a multimillionaire at the same time. You should be ashamed.

Lawrence: Well I'm not ashamed of making a buck. No American is.

I've made some notes since yesterday.

Michael: I might have guessed from that list of faults you started with. The only things you left out. . .

Lawrence: Were the golden parachutes, the greenmail and the poison pills. I know, I'm saving the best. But first let's return to the motivational and monitoring benefits of hostile takeovers. The threat of a takeover has to give a CEO an incentive to perform better, for shareholders and everyone else. It's human nature. Clever argument cannot diminish it.

Michael: Will a surgeon operate better if you keep a gun trained on him? It's a ludicrous reason for takeovers. It's like pilots trying to land 747s with terrorists cavorting in the aisles.

Lawrence: A surgeon and pilot work in controlled environments. A CEO, on the other hand, voluntarily works in an environment that subjects him to market scrutiny and pressure. He gets the rewards. He should bear the burdens. There is no other way to oust him when he messes up.

Michael: We've covered that. The chief flaw in your motivational red herring is the fact that the takeover era only started in 1969. With the Northwest Industries/B.F. Goodrich fight. It didn't get into full swing until about 1974. I wonder how the Republic managed until 1974. This country, this fantastic industrial economy built around public companies and minimal judicial or other government interference. How is it possible that it functioned so well for six or seven decades before the hostile takeover era. Some would say it performed much better in the 1960s. Suddenly you people are talking about the benefits of takeovers as if they were in a class with secret ballots and free speech.

Lawrence: Hostile takeovers started in the late '60s early '70s because there was a need for them. It is part of the economy's periodic restorative process. Some managements were not getting full value out of the assets under their control. It was due primarily to management inability and perhaps in part to general financial conditions -- Federal deficits, inflation and a glum stock market that did not reflect rates of return one could realize from ownership of the assets. The raiders stepped in to correct that. Perfectly natural. Biological, when you think of it.

Michael: And it was never needed before that, right?

Lawrence: I haven't bothered to study earlier periods. Maybe takeovers were needed before, just like the telephone or car were "needed" before they were invented. We have a Rust Belt on our hands now, and I don't think we'd be in such a state if we had had free wheeling takeover activity throughout the 1960s.

Michael: You're like the physicist who comes

up with the theory that can never be tested. If you study what hostile takeover activity there was in America before the late 1960's you'll find that for most of the preceding decades state corporation law actually restricted corporations from making takeovers. To make a takeover by share purchase the raider would have to have risked an antitrust problem. That was because a corporation was not permitted to purchase shares in a company engaged in an unrelated business. This was to insure the investor against the company diversifying, for example a grocery chain going into cosmetics, by means of such an acquisition. If management wanted to buy shares of a company in a different line of business at first they had to go back to the state legislature and get specific permission. Later, they had to at least go back to their own shareholders for approval. Initially it required unanimous approval in some states. So hostile takeovers have never earned an honored place in our economic history. For a long while not even a lawful place.

No, the takeovers we know today and the justification we hear for them are a new device. And they have nothing at all to do with the system correcting itself, or creative destruction, or with assets being undervalued in the market place or with Federal deficit spending or inflation or any of that other sophisticated nonsense. They have to do with customs. With respectability. That is more important than all the laws. Despite relaxation of corporation law restrictions, until the 1970s takeovers were ungentlemanly. They were just not done. Period. They could have been done in the 1960s or 1950s. The duPonts probably could have made a leveraged takeover of IBM in the late 1940s. Would have been a great buy too. You don't have to be smart. All you need is a complete lack of the self restraint that used to keep the tendency to takeover caged up where it belonged, and some financial backers with the same attitude, the same willingness to exploit the jugular in our system. You're right. It is biological, and that's no compliment. This is a question of values, but it's not dollar values, it's human values.

Lawrence: How can you talk about "customs" when we have to deal with threats like foreign competition that didn't really exist before.

Michael: The challenge of foreign competition is a reason to curtail hostile takeovers, because they add nothing to our country's effort to maintain its industrial supremacy. They weaken our position. Like an army in which the incentive is not to leave your bunk, or else to check into the infirmary or the field hospital. Lag it. Why get shot?

Lawrence: Nonsense. Look, I am a firm believer in the "market for corporate control". It's here to stay.

Michael: Whichever economist invented that facile phrase should get a medal from our foreign competitors abroad. It has become a high sounding battle cry for all the people doing harm to America's capitalist structure with these takeovers. As we just saw, it has no heritage whatsoever. It's an intellectual's term for "raids." I read recently where a Federal appellate judge who should know his history kept using it as if it were written somewhere in the U.S. Constitution. This is all part of the myth that accompanies the takeover era. Nothing productive is coming from this. You would think people would stop and say to themselves: If this is such a great thing, how come a small group in and around Wall Street is making all the money from it? How come it hasn't added new jobs? How come it hasn't rejuvenated the productive apparatus? How come it hasn't helped any communities? How come it hasn't increased public tax revenues or lowered prices or improved the quality of goods? Where is all this benefit that we hear about?

Lawrence: These things take time to appear.

Michael: The crowning irony is that just at a time when the two largest socialist nations on earth are beginning to imitate capitalist Western political and social customs, we are permitting home grown opportunists to attack the main vein of America's economic system, the stature and the spirit of its large public business corporations.

Lawrence: What the market for corporate control adds is efficiency . . . which is at the core of our free enterprise system. For example, it's the basis of the efficient market hypothesis? The market knows all, sees all. Absent compelling reasons to think otherwise, a publicly traded company is worth what the market says it is worth, no more, no less. That is why management has an obligation to assist in selling the company when a significant premium over market is offered for it. That's a duty to the shareholders.

Michael: It seems to me that the fact of takeovers refutes your efficient market hypothesis. Moreover, there is respected economic literature to the effect that the efficient market hypothesis was not intended to include management's own special knowledge of the value in the company. Analysis of permitted insider investment returns shows that over a long enough period managers have a better insight about future values in their firms than the market at large. I imagine that's why we have insider trading prohibitions. Management perspective is the exception to the hypothesis, the compelling reason to look beyond the market.

But I don't think the hypothesis weighs heavily in this debate on one side or the other. The issue is not just the proper sale value of a handful of target companies in a year. The issue is performance of all operating independent companies. Operating. Not liquidating, not consolidating, but operating. They can't all be merged but they can all be threatened. The central issue is whether mergers, when they do occur, should be self-initiated and not imposed from without. I think there should be a hard and fast gentleman's understanding — not necessarily a law — that widely held public companies merge only when the people who run them decide they should merge. That's pretty much the way it was in the U.S. We should go back to it. It worked fine. Takeovers developed not because it wasn't working, but because a couple of raiders decided to chart a new way to make a lot of money quickly by ignoring customs. One hesitates to suggest other areas of American life where fortune and fame await those willing to lead such a race.

Lawrence: I still don't think you can prove takeovers are bad because they didn't exist until recently.

By the way, if you regard the long lived, widely held public corporation as such a unique entity, almost an evolutionary event . . .

Michael: That's a fair term for it.

Lawrence: . . . how can you condone its merger out of existence when such an event occurs on a friendly basis? When management initiates it. A merger into another company or a leveraged buy-out by management.

Michael: Because I am trying to be true to the first principle, that for it to work the public company must be self determined. It is its own self-responsibility that gives it its unique character, that makes it capable of great things for society. You can't have that if you rule out the ultimate freedom of its own managers to recommend that it ought to relinquish that autonomous public status. I don't regard those as the happiest of events for society, even though they bring unusual gains to shareholders. One day we will probably see the need to establish stronger disincentives for mergers of public companies above a certain size. We will conclude that our strength, indeed our political safety, is in their numbers. For now, I believe that if a public company's own managers decide -- without duress, immediate or out of the takeover environment, which is the case with all too many LBOs -- if the managers decide to recommend that it should merge into another or go private, then we should not interfere with that if there is full disclosure and if the financial terms are fair by current standards. I concede that the analysis here limps. Beyond the opportunity to attract capital, public status holds great benefits flowing from a large enterprise primarily because of management's freedom to choose, and to plan, and to execute; enforcing public status against the judgment of management might seem to confound the whole process.

Another thing. We still don't really appreciate what occurs when two large companies of long standing merge into one. We know that it is very difficult to make these transactions work, even when they are done with the best of intentions and goodwill on both sides. Look at Mobil and Marcor. At G.E. and Utah International. Exxon and Reliance Electric. The New York Central and the Pennsylvania Railroads. Most large mergers do not work and that is probably because the perceived advantages were primarily financial. In some cases, where they do work, I think what is really going on is not that the surviving company acquired new assets with greater financial promise, but that it attracted new people that it needed to sustain its own mission. A major accounting firm said getting good managers was the leading priority in the negotiated mergers it studied. I can go along with mergers where people are the leading motivation. That's consistent with my respect for the public company. To me, that's a further indication of the unique nature of the public company, an ability to renew itself by reaching out to new human talent. Where you have the smaller public company selling out, making little or no infusion of new management into the acquiror, and perhaps with its own management retiring, there it is much harder to square with my ideas. It seems to be a self annihilation to all outward appearances. It's a problem.

But I suggest you consider this. There are warning signs here and there in the mergers and acquisitions field that should alert us to dangers in this activity. The severe difficulties involved in making any combination of large public companies work is one of those warning signs. That indeed these are not things we are dealing with here, these entities, but something far more complex. We don't understand them. That alone should be a strike against hostile takeovers, where the business

61

combination is done forcibly under the crudest of circumstances. Where the people factor is not only not an opportunity, it's the main hurdle. Way back in 1969, the first public comment by The B.F. Goodrich Company when it was raided by Northwest Industries, the first words of the first press release issued by the first prominent target company of the new takeover era, were: "This is a reckless way to seek to combine large companies." That says it all.

You're pretty fast with pro-takeover slogans. And we have had dozens and dozens of hostile takeovers. Give me one example of a prominent failing company that was in visibly desperate need of improvement and was taken over through a hostile cash offer. A target company that cried out for your more skilled managers to save it by putting its assets to higher uses.

Lawrence: I could cite many examples.

Michael: One will do fine.

Lawrence: Loews Theatres' acquisition of CNA Financial, in 1974.

Michael: That was not what we mean by a hostile takeover. Mr. Tisch and his people had a good look at the books. They even lowered the price in the middle of it. That was a scavenge. I'm interested in the hostile takeovers. The many instances where the raider suddenly shows up from nowhere and stands willing to pay cash for the stock, any and all shares, without any prior access to the books and records, the employees or the properties.

Lawrence: Carl Icahn's bid for TWA.

Michael: Wrong again. Icahn had renegotiated TWA's labor pacts with the unions before he commited himself to the major part of it.

Lawrence: I'd have to review my files, but there certainly are a number of examples.

Michael: If you apologists for the therapeutic value of takeovers had any case at all, the names of prominent targets desperate for takeover and improvement would be tumbling from your lips. We wouldn't be able to keep you quiet. The fact is that it's the relatively sounder companies have been the subjects of all those surprise hostile offers.

And speaking of improving acquired companies, I find it spiritually significant that the hostile takeover that marked the maturity of the modern takeover era, that was supposed to bestow respectability on hostile offers, was International Nickel's 1974 raid on ESB (the former Electric Storage Battery). That's the one where Morgan Stanley made its big splash acting as investment banker for a raider for the first time, you'll recall. Even fearsome United Technologies would only play the role of white knight. There were articles about what an important turning point it was. The young fellow at Morgan Stanley went on to head up a new mergers and acquisitions department at that firm, specializing in hostile takeovers. They made a lot of money. How is ESB doing now Lawrence?

Lawrence: I think INCO wrote it off and closed it, or something like that. But it happens in friendly deals, as well.

Michael: INCO didn't understand the battery business. We could end this discussion right there.

Not only do hostile takeovers not convert failing public companies into good ones. They sometimes convert good ones into failures.

Let's look at another side of all this. Do you think shareholders of raiding companies are being treated fairly?

Lawrence: I don't understand the question.

Michael: Now that corporation laws have been relaxed, do raider CEOs check with their shareholders before they pop off and make a hostile tender offer?

Lawrence: It would compromise secrecy.

Michael: I assume you think raider management should also be accountable to someone?

Lawrence: Definitely.

Michael: But you would let them embark on drastic changes in their companies through acquisitions without any requirement that they consult these owners of the shares that you say you feel so deeply about. Why wouldn't one of the biggest objections to hostile takeovers made by other large operating companies be that the management of the raiding company doesn't know what it's buying? They haven't had a look at the books. You can't buy a large public company just on the basis on the public financials. Those are trading market financials, not acquisition financials. You have to get the details of the labor agreements, of the pension plans, of the customer and supplier long term contracts. You have to know more about the tax accounting picture. Most of all you have to know the people. It is fitting to describe a surprise takeover as recklessness on the part of the raider's management. Here they are spending the corporation's money, and they don't know what they are really buying. It's an ego trip. Look at the details in a typical friendly merger agreement between two public companies. Look at all the assurances that are given regarding the items I mentioned, and all the opportunity the buyer has to go in with lawyers and accountants and check up on whether the assurances are accurate. All of that is a waste of time if hostile takeovers are a prudent and reasonable method of doing an acquisition. Now where it's a private raider spending his own money on a hostile takeover — or rather spending the junk bond money raised for him -- maybe if he wants to act recklessly that's his business although other people can still get hurt. But when you have a public company playing the raider role, management should have a real conflict there under your theory. Or could it be that they endeavor to reduce that conflict by buying only sound but undervalued businesses. You see the dilemma in your position there don't you?

We are fortunate that we have had only a handful of public company raiders. That's another of the warning signs about takeovers. There is something about the complex process that selects a CEO, and I don't mean only the final action of the directors but also the entire career process, there is something about it that seems to select ones whose makeup tells them hostile takeovers are not an acceptable way to do business. It is the rare CEO of a large company who will make a hostile offer.

Lawrence: That's changing.

Michael: No, it is not changing. It's constant.

It's not changing.

By the way, what do you think of a prominent raider CEO recommending to his public shareholders that they vote to transform the company into a limited partnership that has only two general partners — the CEO and a dummy company owned by the CEO? Where he will have absolute, dictatorial decision-making authority in all matters, not even a board of directors to worry about?

Lawrence: That seems excessive. But maybe he's an unusually astute gentleman who needn't be subject to the normal disciplines.

Michael: The finely drawn double standard in all its glory. "I like raiders because they punish businessmen, who I don't like. Therefore, raider CEOs can ignore the shareholders. In fact they can form limited partnerships and effectively eliminate the shareholders. They're the good guys so I'll let them do that." How can you go about saying this drivel?

Lawrence: You said it. You're starting to play both roles now. Raiders can be taken over, too —like Bendix — and thus are subject to the same disciplines. So raiders have to perform well too.

Michael: But you don't mind as much if they erect ultimate management entrenchment schemes.

Lawrence: As long as they submit the proposal to their shareholders for prior approval, no, I don't mind that.

Michael: I'm glad we got that on the record. And then there's the biggest warning sign of all in takeovers — the professional wrestlers that get all the attention. Don't they just personify the worthlessness and the harm of the activity?

Lawrence: Wrestlers?

Michael: You know, the investment bankers and lawyers who parade around as if they are contesting these things.

Lawrence: We have to have them and their expertise don't we?

Michael: Your arbs created them. They got their start because arbitrageurs — usually unnamed — were quoted in the media as saying how great they are. The arbs taught the lawyers, the arbs and the lawyers taught the investment bankers. It's ironic that a company would hire a takeover advisor because the arbitrageurs are impressed with him.

Lawrence: The arbitrageurs are professionals -- the top of the line in the takeover business. They recognize ability better than anyone. What's wrong with that?

Michael: What's wrong with it is that if a company is to ward off a bid and stay independent, by definition the arbitrageurs are going to lose money. If a company is going to buy another company, it wants to get a bargain, which means the arbs aren't going to make as much money. Why should a CEO ever want advisors the arbs recommend for heavens sake?

Lawrence: Because it takes an expert to know an expert, and these advisors have a duty of loyalty to their client. You get some of these traditional law firms involved, for example, or a classical banker, and they're all thumbs. You need a real pro.

Michael: That's never been important. For example, your experts have uniformly poor records at defending companies confronted with a cash takeover bid. Their knowledge is limited to intricate superficialities. The only thing that differentiates them is that they are cozy with the arbs and the rest of the takeover crowd. They get all sorts of publicity without really doing anything except being on the scene making insignificant noise when companies are taken over. They're like a Greek chorus. CEOs are talked into thinking you can't have a takeover fight without the chorus so they hire them.

Lawrence: Are you talking about lawyers or investment bankers now?

Michael: There's not much difference. If you tried to write a biography of one of those fellows it would be hard to do. They haven't accomplished anything notable other than "being there" and getting incredible press. I guess that would have to be the story line. How they got such press by doing so little. You could call it "The Self Promoter's Story." They are so firmly established now that if you read a news item about one of their younger generation, it will say he has advised on 50 takeovers. That means he was there. But did he advise a target that escaped a cash offer? Or a raider that won even though a third company was offering a higher price? Never. His job is to be there. The takeover community is in good hands when he's there. No one will do anything dangerous that could cost the community a lot of cash, on the pending deal or as precedent in future deals.

Lawrence: You think that the CEOs who have hired these people are foolish, yet in all other business decisions the CEOs are reasonably astute.

Michael: CEOs have been gulled here because of the complexity of the area and their ingrained trust of the financial press and of Wall Street firms. For generations people in those firms earned that trust. To the point where trying to tell some CEOs what's really going on now would be like trying to persuade them their minister is a wife beater. But I think they are catching on, slowly.

Lawrence: You accused me of bias. You don't care for hostile takeovers. That doesn't give you the right to indict all the experts who make their living on hostile takeovers.

Michael: As a supporter of the independent public company, I hold them accountable for their gross insincerity. If you can find one who is sincere, I'll respect him.

Lawrence: What do you mean by sincere?

Michael: A lawyer, for example, who tells the client, or the press if asked, "Look, I can't do a thing to keep a target company independent. I can file frivolous lawsuits and cause a lot of excitement that entertains the press. But I've been on the defending side in scores of these and I haven't been able to stop a single one. The ones that are stopped once in a long while are stopped by antitrust injunctions. I'm not even an antitrust lawyer, so don't look to me for that. If you want to hire me, I know all the slang words and I have a file of forms of the documents you will need. But rest assured the outcome is preordained. You get yourself a funded cash takeover bid for more than a majority of the shares and you're gone. You'll lose your independence or your financial stability for certain." I'll respect the takeover lawyer who says that, and who does not take public credit for gimmicks he copied and that that have no final bearing on the outcome of a takeover fight. I'll also respect the investment banker who says to the potential target company: "If you become the target of a cash raid, don't look to me to keep you independent in your present financial condition. We can't do a thing. Get a good antitrust lawyer. The government may be going softer on antitrust, but there's no sign the Federal courts are. However, if you decide that you want to get a higher price for the shares, then I think my firm -- given enough time -- can do as good a job as anyone checking with possible white knights who might pay more money than the raider. We're good at that. Or we can help you escape, if you want to call it that, by shooting yourself in the leg with a burdensome financial restructuring". I'll respect that fellow too.

My problem with all of these people is that they strut around taking credit for this, that and the other thing, basking in their celebrity status and charging excessive fees. When in fact they are just unimportant supporting cast, feeding the views of the arbs and other speculators into the monotonous drama of highest cash price offered in time wins. Always. These takeover advisors don't have any effect on the outcome. No, I take that back. They don't have any effect of the kind the client is looking for. I'm afraid they frequently do have the opposite effect. That is, if the client is the target company, these people not only don't keep it independent, I think their presence on the scene facilitates the company losing its independence. For example, they will argue impatiently. "Let's get started with the white knights" when unexciting regular company counsel is trying to put together an antitrust case against the raider. Things like that. Also, they are much too accessible to the press. They're the ones that always account for the quotes from unnamed sources that the target is "gearing up for a real fight" or that it has "arranged large lines of credit" or that "the directors are meeting Sunday" or that "the company has hired ABC law firm" or "XYZ investment bankers". The arbitrageurs _love_ stories like this. They spell "money, money, money . . . come and get it." They stir the feeding frenzy, that forces the company onto the auction block. What worries the arbs is silence.

If the client is a buyer, a raider, I'm sure the presence of the takeover professionals at his elbow leads to him having to pay more for the target. Executives don't stop to notice that these so called fights always end up the same. Go back to the United Technologies takeover bid for Babcock & Wilcox in 1977 and look at the record for the next 10 years, or say contests concluded through September 1986. You'll find that about 55 hard fought hostile cash takeover bids were made for large companies that hadn't already teed themselves up by announcing a management LBO or a tender offer for their own shares. Six a year, and that's about how they were spread out. How many of those targets remained independent, in the same financial condition as before?

Lawrence: Not many.

Michael: One, that's all. Grumman. And it was because they won an antitrust injunction against LTV. And they didn't rely on a takeover law firm to do that either. Five kept their independence only through radical restructuring that could have

71

impaired the company's financial and operating condition. Twenty-five were driven into the arms of a white knight, and the other twenty-four were acquired by the original raider. There were three more that escaped because the raider decided against the thing on its own, before a formal cash offer was ever started. I don't count them as determined hostile offers.

It's incredible that against that record people can go around bragging in interviews and newspaper ads "Hire me, hire my firm for the defense." And that the press consistently describes these fakers as experts at defense, lawyers and investment bankers both. The only smart defensive steps are taken before a bid is made. They never attract any publicity. The successful takeover defenses are ones you never read about. Much of defense involves knowing who to stay away from in Wall Street. Once a hostile cash offer is made, there have been no experts at defense.

Large investment banking firms now have an unhealthy financial stake in continued takeover activity. They publish contrived studies showing that a substantial percentage of target companies escape raids. This perpetuates the myth that these things can be defeated and that there is someone in New York you should hire if you become a target. When you analyze the studies -- which some pillars of the financial press have failed to do — you see that they are grossly misleading. They include deals that were not hard fought hostile cash takeovers. I've given you the real statistics. If you count a white knight merger as a loss of the public company's idependence, as you must, the target company won — lost record for the 10 years was: Wins - 1, Losses -49, Withdrew because of injury - 5.

When the takeover professionals are not involved in deals they seem to spend all their time working to faciliate more takeover activity. Attorneys at firms supposedly noted for defensive assignments will publish articles and make speeches attacking the validity of state laws designed to help companies ward off takeovers. At every turn they want more Federal regulation of business, less authority in the states. Federal authorities have been sympathetic toward takeovers. Takeover attorneys concoct the most outrageous schemes that cause the courts to narrow the state law concept of the business judgment rule. The historic rule that gives businessmen the benefit of the doubt.

Prominent investment bankers serve on a special government committee that recommends restrictions against corporate charter clauses that moderate takeovers, and relaxation of traditional disclosure procedures so as to allow all paper takeovers — the ones where the raider prints his own money — to proceed as rapidly as cash offers. They testify at Congressional hearings against extending the disallowance of the interest deduction, telling Congressional committees with a straight face that the interest deduction has nothing to do with takeovers.

People can worry about celebrated insider trading scandals growing out of takeovers, but I think the country can survive a series of those. Where the irreparable damage is being done is from inside the major investment banking and law firms, in their relationships to their clients. If a whole new ethic has taken hold, if it becomes firm policy to mislead the client company, pull the wool over its eyes as to one's real abilities and objectives — and worse, gently nudge the trusting client into a takeover situation, or nudge it from a minor flare up into an all out bidding contest, just so the firm can make a big fee. If we have that kind of dealing going on, then we have serious problems, very serious problems. The whole vaunted liquidity mechanism has become fouled.

Lawrence: Often a client doesn't know what it wants. The advisors have been there before so they can do what they were hired to do — advise the company as to what's best for shareholders. Nothing nefarious is going on.

Michael: I don't agree, based on a lot of circumstantial evidence — the chronology of each takeover, the pattern of it, viewed from my experience, my study of this area for many years.

Lawrence: You've made oblique references to the press in our talks. As if you think the press is gullible, or worse, as if there is an unholy alliance with the takeover interests.

Michael: Someone once noticed that the financial press is unlike the general press, because it is more than a matter of our interest. We are likely to act upon it.

Many members of the financial press are a little partial to seeing management catch it in the slats. The takeover advisors have no doubt appeared to be the instruments of that. I think that this sentiment among the press has eclipsed a more important function we expect from them — the unmasking of people who are not what they pretend to be. The press must know as well as you know that these takeover professionals don't make any difference at all except to keep the show running lucratively. Yet they write about them as if they were Green Berets, when as I say they are really right out of the World Wrestling Federation. That's what I have a problem with. Editorial writers in the press are entitled to extoll the benefits of takeovers. As Schumpeter noticed, intellectuals have always demonstrated an antipathy toward the business class. But when what should be editorial creeps into the news columns, in the form of articles advertising these mercenary advisors in a way that causes trusting CEOs and directors to seek to hire them, open the gates to them and give them full control in takeovers, that's where I have a problem.

Nine-tenths of everything that is written about hostile takeovers -- not just in the daily press but in articles and books on the subject, non-fiction and fiction -- has no basis in reality. It portrays instead the conditions that the takeover community wishes portrayed, conditions conducive to further profits by them. It's amazing how successful they have been with the media.

Lawrence: You have steered clear of the historical record in the U.S. Congress. Congress decided way back in 1968 that there should be a "level playing field" in takeovers and . . .

Michael: That's a buzz word like "market for corporate control". I don't think you'll find it anywhere in the legislative history. Pro-takeover economists and judges love it, but some latter-day apologist made it up.

Lawrence: Anyway, Congress decided it did not want to tip the scales against hostile takeovers. That's a pretty impressive endorsement of them.

This whole thing was looked at years ago and it was decided, after hearings, that takeovers were a positive thing and that we should not forbid them.

Michael: What Congress did in 1968 was decide that takeovers should not go completely unregulated, while proxy fights which we have discussed had been closely regulated for thirty years. So Congress required a few procedural rules for tender offers -- like giving people some time to decide — and also some minimum disclosures, such as the identity of the bidder, his source of financing and his plans for the target company. That's all Congress did. The states would have done it if Congress hadn't. Virginia already had. If you read some articles and judicial opinions you would think Congress studied these takeovers closely and approved of them, which is wrong. It never did.

The fact is Congress couldn't have decided there was good in takeovers because Congress would have been ahead of itself. Hostile takeovers weren't even out of their cave in 1968. Congress wasn't in a position then to draw conclusions about the kind of bedlam of takeovers we have with us today. Congress acted in 1968 because of a few egregious examples of what senior Senators thought were abuses. In a very backhanded way the committee reports referred to <u>not</u> tipping the balance of regulation. What they actually said was that "it was urged" that takeovers not be discouraged because they serve a useful purpose and the legislation "avoids" that. Not "we hereby decide that" but "it was urged that". This is a far cry from an endorsement of hostile takeovers. Congress has never deliberated the broad questions of the good and ill in hostile takeovers. That subject has not come up yet in any formal way. There have been rumblings, statements made that appear to be intended to appeal to special interest constituents, but no serious attention to it. Sooner or later it must happen. The country, our entire economic and social system is being damaged by these things, and it is necessary to analyze them. See what they really are.

Lawrence: I'm glad to hear you admit that Congress believes takeovers "serve a useful purpose." In my view, that's all that really needs to be said.

Michael: You're not even listening.

Again, the businessman's lot will never be respected by the general populace. For reasons that can be followed far back into our history and our cultural heritage, and that have to do with the difficulty in seeing the long range benefits in a complex economic system, one that arouses little emotional attachment. On the contrary it arouses a certain resentment perhaps due to distant genetic memories of a reluctant shift from agrarian to urban life. Because of this atmosphere, I see an overriding obligation of responsible political leaders to speak out and to moderate anti-business sentiment in public debate when it grows extreme, such as that which accompanies the present takeover movement. We need a political and social climate that is deferential to large public companies if we are to have economic prosperity. It's that simple. Elected representatives have a duty to understand this, to rise above the usual short term considerations in politics, and to challenge those who would exploit our valuable system of independent public companies for personal gain. It is sad to read some of the comments made by U.S. Senators and Representatives at occasional legislative hearings on this topic. They play to the same anti-business inclinations that you and your pals

77

do. They should know better.

The have-nots in society never enter into a discussion of hostile takeovers, but those who do not yet enjoy the prosperity of our economy, their chance of ever participating depends on this climate toward business more than any other factor. More than all other factors put together. In the end, we will probably see legislation, state or Federal, that will recognize the importance of what is at stake here and that will make these hostile takeovers more difficult to accomplish. We might not.

Lawrence: Every time there is a major breakout of takeovers into a new field, like oil companies, everybody runs to Washington and hollars for new legislation. I'll never forget nine or ten years ago the head of a large company urged Senator Kennedy's antitrust subcommittee to pass a law that said simply "Hostile mergers, or acquisitions, are prohibited." Last year that same CEO finally resigned his position amid growing public outcry about management perquisites and favoritism at his company and sharply declining profits. Legislation against takeovers would be a bad thing. No one has even figured out what kind of legislation would work.

Michael: I'm not sure Federal legislation is going to be the answer either. Respectability is the answer. As the Scottish politician said,"he cared not who writes a country's laws if he could write its songs."

I do hope to see it made clearer, at least, that states have broad authority to legislate in this takeover area. If the state where a company is incorporated wants to regulate a takeover of that company, I'd let it. Thirty seven states have tried to do that and Federal courts -- not Congress but Federal courts -- have told them they can't. That was wrong. Very wrong. You can't tell 37 states to go jump when their legislatures have studied the question and the issues on the merits, and Congress never studied the thing at all. Lately the Supreme Court is coming around to this point of view, and at least affirming the jurisdiction of states over the goverance of their own domestic corporations, even where that conflicts with takeovers. Congress should now specifically recognize that the states have authority to regulate tender offers for control of public companies created, and perhaps even principally situated in the state. If that interferes with the interstate "market for corporate control," then good. That so called "market" is only about 12 years old. It is an excess of the infatuation with liquidity. It hasn't done anyone any good except an opportunistic few and it would be good to abolish it so that we can get on with the Nation's business without this wasteful takeover distraction.

Lawrence: The states also were the ones to block civil rights and other things, so you can't rely on the state legislatures as being all prudent. Everyone knows the states will do the bidding of the large local companies. That's why we need Washington in the middle of this.

Michael: Well, its clear that the record of attempted Federal regulation of hostile tender offers has been a sorry one. It started out with promise in 1968 because SEC staffers then understood that Congress meant to rein these things in, not endorse them. But after 10 years the SEC's attitude changed. The Commission started to adopt curious rules that facilitated and protected takeover activity. For example, a rule designed to override any state regulation of tenders. And a rule exempting arbitrageurs from having to disclose their securities positions like other managers of large portfolios. Leading takeover advisors and speculators were invited to come down and participate in an SEC advisory panel. Then some Federal court decisions in the last two years turned the whole regulatory structure on its head. Congress never defined what a "tender offer" was. The courts should have given the term a liberal scope, picking up any manner of stock accumulation that avoids putting one's acquisition proposal before all the shareholders on an equal basis. Instead the courts have given the term "tender offer" an excessively narrow meaning. First they let a person buy 10% or 15% of a company in the stock market without having to follow the tender offer procedures laid down in 1968. Lately they are letting people buy nearly 50% in the stock market, all in one fell swoop. Purchases made without any of the procedural safeguards Congress wanted in change of control share acquisitions. No right of withdrawal. No treatment of sellers on a pro rata basis. There is no need to make a formal tender offer any more. Just buy the stock when you feel like it.

Today Federal regulation is a complete shambles. As a result of a little understood Supreme Court ruling it is even questionable whether the SEC had statutory authority to adopt many of its more recent rules, including a rule that everyone thinks applies to the latest insider trading scandals. Personally, I think this chaos is yet one more warning sign of the real underlying problem with hostile tender offers. They are intrinsically negative activity. You will be confounded if you try to regulate them as if there were anything positive there. It can't be done. Foul practices will continue to pour forth like a Niagara Falls.

In constitutional practice there is a respected view that the states can serve as useful laboratories for the Federal government. This is an ideal situation for application of that philosophy. Since things have come apart so badly at the Federal level nearly two decades later, let's not have different Federal regulation. That would likely wind up being aimed back at business rather than at takeovers, given Wall Street's success record in the Congress. Let's turn the entire area over to the states. Maybe some or all of them can come up with a sensible regulatory format. The Federal government can adopt it later. This delegation or acquiesence in state authority works well for insurance regulation, and insurance is a great deal more important than takeovers are. The only thing standing in the way of this approach is the moronic notion of an interstate "market for corporate control." There is no reason to protect so-called interstate markets in novel activities that do harm to the fabric of society.

I'm not saying that Federal legislation is needed. There are ways the states can regulate takeovers in a meaningful way without changing the cases already decided by the Federal courts. They can regulate the terms of mergers. North Carolina has recently passed the most sophisticated statute in the country on this subject. It completely eliminates the stampede element that all hostile takeovers depend on. States might also return to the old system and prohibit their creatures from buying stocks in other companies. I wonder what the "market for corporate control" advocates would say to that. As for other legislation, the most effective thing Congress could do is to extend the 1969 Wilbur Mills bill so it covers interest on any debt used for hostile offers, not just the convertible debt.

81

Lawrence: The tax committee staffers have looked at that and they say it can't be done. You can't separate out the unfriendly from the friendly deals in a tax code section. It sounds easy but it isn't.

Michael: It can be done. The tax technicians in Congress don't understand enough about how friendly mergers differ from hostile ones. It would be very easy to write an amendment to section 279 of the Internal Revenue Code (the Mills Bill) that continues to allow interest deductions for debt used in negotiated leveraged buyouts and negotiated mergers, but disallows it for deals where the buyer acquires shares of a public company. Only takes about 20 words.

Lawrence: I don't think Congress will ever do that. What Wilbur Mills' bill did in 1969, that was rare. It caught us off guard and you're right, it did set back takeovers 10 to 15 years. But next time we'll be ready. Since 1978, every two years there has been a rash of headlines like "Backlash Against Takeovers Seen Growing" or "Congress Expected to Curb Takeovers" or "Business Stepping Up Opposition to Raiders." But nothing happens. The takeovers go merrily along, and get bigger and bigger. It's wonderful.

Michael: If you want to get controversial, I'd even consider putting a lid on the size of these institutional investors, these fund managers. I'm not sure, but they might have too much power already, and their purely market price orientation is extremely unhealthy. Either that or I'd have the states limit their right to vote, adjust the voting power of stock to the length of time it has been held by the investor. You moan about unaccountability of management. Some of our largest companies are coming under the actual voting control of 75 to 100 people --hired hands employed by institutions that don't actually own a single share of the stock for their own account. That kind of concentration, which is itself diversified, coupled with the lack of familiarity with the controlled enterprise, the lack of responsibility for it, the lack of clear standards of success or failure, the lack of inhibitions against reckless behavior. It's not good. It loses touch with reality. The raider/reformers are starting to play to this audience now and it is likely to get out of hand. If the institutions could find some effective way to flow votes through to the real parties in interest, to the workers who are represented by these large pension funds, and to let workers shape the institutions' attitudes toward takeovers, then the present voting system will probably work for a while longer. But if the votes are going to continue to be cast by these money managers, then there's a big problem there.

Lawrence: You're not just trying to stop takeovers. You're trying to make fundamental changes in the system, going way beyond takeovers.

Michael: On the contrary, I'm trying to prevent fundamental and far reaching shifts in the way the system has worked if it's necessary to contain these takeovers. That's the only motive. What I would like to see is recognition deeply rooted in our society --as indeed it was before 1969 -- that our large public companies are not something that can be monetized, batted about, and auctioned off for a quick profit by irresponsible speculators in the financial community. That is not what auction markets exist for in the first place. These companies are one of our most valuable national assets and we have to guard them from that at all costs. You ask a sophisticated foreign businessman some day, ask him what he admires, envies, most about America. He just might say it is our large public corporations. I've heard that. It's an extremely perceptive observation. We have something truly wonderful here, and we better appreciate it.

Lawrence: You're carrying water on both shoulders. You say you welcome proxy fights. . .

Michael: I don't exclude them, not for now.

Lawrence: . . . but you would cut back on the right of large funds to vote.

Michael: For the duration, I'm still willing to go with old fashioned proxy fights, even letting the funds vote their shares. If these corporate governance rabblerousers keep up their antics, however, then yes I'd favor reining in those institutions that vote their stock so as to precipitate a takeover. At that stage I would have grave questions about proxy contests unless something were done along these lines. I assume you would prefer restrictions on voting to restrictions on resale absent a material adverse change in the holder's circumstances.

Lawrence: Since I know you favor new investment of savings in capital assets, I'll pretend I didn't hear that last remark. I think you're being inconsistent. Either you allow the record holder to vote or you are interfering with proxy contests.

Michael: The guiding principle in all this, to my mind, is that long standing public companies do not merge out of existence except for reasons that spring from within. Anything that threatens that principle, whether it be raiders, speculators or large institutional holders casting other peoples' votes to tee a company up — I'm opposed.

Here while I worry about the long range consequences of these fund managers having a vote, the takeover crowd is pushing in the opposite direction. Key spokesmen are starting a public campaign, the unstated goal of which is to turn all the pension funds into arbs. And to separate them from the corporate employer's control.

Lawrence: I know about that program. The goals is to reform the proxy system, to achieve better management accountability.

Michael: Sure. And the Russians were invited into Afghanistan by the local leaders. These stalking horses for the takeover crowd are maneuvering to neutralize the one leverage that public companies might have over fund managers. They hire them. They pay their salaries. Not that company A hires managers for a pension fund that owns company A stock. The pension laws limit the amount of stock of the employer company that can be held in the company's own pension plan. We should set aside a whole day to talk about the questionable value judgements implicit in that rule some time.

Lawrence: It's a prudent man rule. What's wrong with it?

Michael: A company is sound enough for someone to spend their whole career there. But not sound enough to stand surety for their retirement income?

Lawrence: It's at the heart of our entire corporate pension system. It's at the heart of trust and fiduciary law too.

Michael: So what. It's wrong. But we're getting off the subject.

Company A hires managers to invest its pension fund, so they buy stocks of Companies B, C and D. The other companies do likewise. What the takeover crowd would like to do is unleash the might of those billions in pension funds in a gigantic takeover orgy. The pension funds would gang up behind some arb-raider type and use their voting power to force management to either restructure or find a buyer for the company. They'd elect their own directors to do it if management wouldn't. The pension funds would also commit to buy the junk bonds that would have to be used to finance the threatened takeovers, thereby giving the arb-raider the club he needs to get the action going. And of course they would arbitrage the target's stock. Wall Street would displace Las Vegas. It would be paved with gold. For the takeover crowd, which would now embrace the fund managers.

Lawrence: You're fantasizing. That's paranoia.

Michael: There's the one catch in all this. The company managements collectively still get to pick the managers of the pension funds collectively. And historically managements have always been able to look at proxy cards and see how shareholders are voting. Investors have never cared about these non-secret ballots. But the takeover community now wants to change that, and although they will make speeches about the little investor, it isn't for the little investor's benefit. They want a secret ballot process. Then the head of company A, when the funds who own his company's stock are voting to force a takeover at his annual meeting, won't be able to call up the head of company D and C and D who hired those people to invest their pension funds and say "Look what these guys are doing. They're using your company's pension fund to take our company over." The takeover crowd and some of the fund managers are rightly concerned that CEOs aren't going to sit still for that. So they want to hide the results of the voting. That only partially solves the problem. What they most want to do is take away management's power to select the trustees. That will be the ultimate in the separation of the ownership of stock from the voting of stock.

Lawrence: You're seeing ghosts.

Michael: I don't think so. I've watched this crowd for so long, I can see their next moves before they can. That's where they are going. All this populist appeal in public to the little shareholder is propaganda. As far as the takeover crowd is concerned, the little shareholder could dry up and blow away.

Lawrence: You forget that the U.S. Government through the Department of Labor encourages all of this activity by the fund managers.

Michael: Yes. I know. I'm troubled by that. The DOL policy makers may mean well, but they are way off the reservation. Congress should look into it. The close parallels between the objectives of the DOL and of the takeover crowd are disturbing. The DOL was never intended to be playing this kind of a role in our economy. They are in a position today to affect the wave of corporate takeovers. If the takeover crowd has its way they may be in a position to influence the selection of the managers of these giant pension funds. The consequences of that are startling.

I know of one situation where they came into a takeover involving an ERISA matter and acted like they were an arbitrageur instead of an agency of the U.S. Government. They were throwing around slang lines like the company was "in play" and attacking the "entrenched management." It was shocking to see it, especially from people who know absolutely nothing about the takeovers.

Lawrence: The best system is a prudent man rule, with a fiduciary duty to make the highest return while being prudent. You said legislation may not be the answer and we agree on that, for different reasons. What is the answer, in your view, so I can tell my friends?

Michael: Respectability. Until now business has been floundering around in the face of the takeovers. One company is attacked by predators and all the others stand there, thankful it wasn't their turn. Docile. Like Greeks in the Cyclops cave, waiting to be devoured. Although takeovers are the ultimate business matter, managements have not taken the time away from business matters to learn enough about takeovers. They rely entirely on outside experts. This gives the raiders and the often insincere advisors an opportunity they shouldn't have. The whole financial and legal system, the liquidity dome, that brings us the takeovers is supported primarily by the normal day to day patronage of the large public companies. The takeover machine makes a fortune from takeovers, but it can't subsist on takeovers alone. The commercial banks, investment bankers, pension funds and large law offices — they all depend on the custom of operating public companies. If the top executives of those companies understood the takeover shenanigans better, that alone would cause the financial and legal community to back off. It would amount to starting to put back in the cage the wild thing that got loose around the time of the International Nickel — ESB takeover.

Lawrence: I don't believe this. You would have business boycott the financial community to stop the takeovers?

Michael: Not really a boycott, necessarily. Education is the main thing. Once CEOs understand what really goes on in takeovers, how they actually originate, and what the real role of the advisors is, I'm hopeful the rest will follow like the night the day. Maybe everyone will just agree that the takeovers should be stopped. I don't rule that out. I hope to persuade you of that.

Lawrence: We haven't talked about the regulation of trading. My own view is the less regulation on trading the better -- that's the way it is abroad.

Michael: Insider trading staged a breakout with the arrival of hostile takeovers. It won't subside until you check the takeovers. You cannot have hostile takeovers and not have rampant insider trading. They go together like dollars and cents. By definition, when you have people secretly planning assaults on other people you will have insider trading. What's even worse, when you have investment banking firms and law firms standing to make huge fees if their "clients" are assaulted, you will have a more insidious kind of insider trading that creates the necessary appearance of an assault in the offing.

Hostile takeovers should not be banned just because of insider trading. That's a poor reason, the tail wagging the dog. But Congress must appreciate it will always have insider trading unless it decides to restrict the takeovers. It better get used to these scandals otherwise. Another of our warning signs.

Lawrence: The whole concept of insider trading is an economic experiment run amuck. We need efficient securities markets. That means we need to let the markets digest all information, not just certain information that happens to have been publicly disclosed already. If we have to choose between disclosure and efficiency, I'd go for the efficiency. There is a direct conflict there.

Michael: I agree with you. There's a conflict, and it's not black and white. My own feeling is that you can have the most efficient markets possible, but if average investors don't trust them, they will be less active markets. "Fool me twice, shame on me" -- that idea. If they become less active, then to that extent they become less efficient.

Lawrence: I don't understand the regulatory philosophy behind the insider trading rules. I thought that fifty years ago Congress decided you could not regulate insider trading. You couldn't track it all down, couldn't prove the cases.

Michael: And most state courts then found nothing wrong with an insider, such as a director, making a profit at the expense of a shareholder who was unaware of some development. As long as the director didn't hurt the interests of the company.

Lawrence: So Congress instead took the practical approach and chose what someone called a "crude rule of thumb." If you are a corporate director or officer or 10% shareholder and you make an in and out (or out and in) profit within 6 months, bam — you have to pay it back to the company. No excuses allowed. No criminal liability either. Just get out your checkbook. Now, fifty years later, the SEC and the prosecutors are pursuing what you can only call a finely tuned rule to snare insider trading. It's so finely tuned that no one can understand it anymore. It's gotten out of hand.

You can't say advance word of a news article is inside information. That's preposterous. And these people that speculate on takeover tips. I would regulate them as if they were part of the bidder's camp. But you can't call those tips inside information. The whole scheme needs to be rethought.

Michael: As I said, I don't link the insider trading thing with my objection to the takeovers. They are separate issues, although takeovers are an optimal breeding ground for insider trading rumors.

For those who would curb insider trading, the role of the press has to come in for some thoughtful reexamination too. For example, advisors who did insider trading, they needed access to confidential information and control over events in order to do it. They needed access to the decision makers, those who could influence market prices. The financial press built up advisors with ridiculous great man articles. That put their firms in a limelight where CEOs believed they must hire them. Because the press kept saying they were essential. Once in the executive suite, some unscrupulous persons in those firms were in a position to influence events and work their schemes. The question is: Did they supplant traditional advisors who might have kept clients' confidences. Similarly the press built up certain takeover speculators, magnifying their capacity to engage in wrongdoing.

One of the things that makes a free press so valuable, our only sure line of defense against tyrants, especially in what we think is a democracy, is that as individuals we can whale away at it when it falls asleep. That happened with the takeover insider scandals.

Lawrence: We need a strong arbitrage community to make our securities markets function efficiently. I am concerned that insider trading witch hunts will weaken the arbitrage business.

Michael: Agreed. We do need arbitrage, even the risk arbitrage which seeks to profit from differences in proposed merger prices and actual market prices of public companies to be acquired. If the investor owns shares in a company that is to be acquired at a certain value, but there are conditions before it will occur, he should be able to sell into a competitive market where the trading price reflects skilled analysis of the proposed acquisition price discounted for those yet unsatisfied conditions. Arbitrageurs make that market for the investor. I would just like to see them confined to working the uncertainties in friendly deals. There would be more of them if we didn't have hostile deals. And there would be just as much money to be made by the most able.

Lawrence: Yesterday you said the number of people who make hostile offers will always be limited.

Michael: Offers for large companies, yes.

Lawrence: It seems to me it is spreading, which is a good development.

Michael: I doubt it. Just look at that junk bond war chest Icahn threatened Phillips Petroleum with. Four to five billion. That same financing was taken from one takeover to another after that time, and waved over managements' heads to prompt them to restructure or run to a white knight. Each time the proposed financial backers earned a commitment fee, but they never had to put up their cash. One of these days the available war chest will be called upon. They'll make a bid for the wrong large company, and the management will wheel on them and say "you got it." That actually happened recently in a takeover of a tool and equipment company. And then the planned asset sales won't pencil out and so the junk money pool won't replenish itself. Eventually I think the Drexel junk bond financing might dry up for the large hostile takeovers. It might not. Those fellows that use it have gotten a lot of mileage out of the same tires. It can't go on like that, I don't think. Unless, of course, there is a sea change and the prominent pension funds and insurance companies start paying cash for the junk debt and putting it in their "prudent man" portfolios. That's possible.

Lately, the last few years, we have seen the rise of the arbs-turned-raiders, the so-called corporate control entrepreneurs. They use shells and they're entirely dependent on the junk financing. As I see it that's a built in limitation.

There is still such a dearth of raids that in the last year arbs and investment bankers seem to have engineered a "bathtub" conspiracy to persuade companies to buy back stock without a raider even surfacing. It's great! You have eliminated the need to have a raider!

Take a minute and notice the progression here. As we entered the 1980s there were too few takeovers to suit the arbs and the takeover crowd. Because there are so few large companies that will jump on their neighbors with hostile takeovers. A head of mergers at a large investment firm would see it as a gymnasium floor packed with gerbils. They are all peaceful. It takes one mad gerbil to start a fight. Once a fight starts, the banker can get lots of other gerbils to come to the rescue, and help carry off the victim, and the banker's firm makes a fee. But none of these rescurer gerbils would ever start something. So everyone sits around waiting for someone to start it. A bad guy. Think back over the years. How many large company bad guys have we seen? People of enormous ego who wanted to be in the Fortune top 50, have bigger salaries, more jet planes, and couldn't do it through friendly acquisitions. The takeover community overcame part of that problem when they invented the arb-raider. It's like an accident lawyer arranging his own accidents. It's Heisenberg's principle of indeterminacy at play in yet another context: no longer is the arb measuring the deal. The arb is the deal. These new style raiders are euphemistically called "corporate control entrepreneurs" by the intellectuals. They may not be arbs formally, but that's all they are. Instead of speculating on someone else's takeover, they buy stock and then use junk bond promises to create their own takeover and speculate on that. A business school professor who should know better has compared them to artists. They are thick with the regular arbs. I think they were created by the arbs, and are aimed by them. The common goal is to start the feeding frenzy. Tee a big company up, and then everyone makes money.

What these arb-raiders are doing today was described exactly by one of their forebearers writing of certain financial practices a century ago. I brought this with me. It is quoted in Samuel Eliot Morison's The Oxford History of the American People. You'll think the fellow who wrote this was alive today when you hear it:

> "At this period Americans found they could, by the exercise of a daring and cunning of a peculiar, reckless and low order, so take advantage of the laws of the land and its economic customs as to create for themselves wealth, or the equivalent, money, to practically an unlimited extent, without the aid of time or labor or the possession of any unusual ability coming through birth or education".

Maybe our own history will record that the final straw was when the arb raiders appeared. No longer were takeovers spurred by businessmen, albeit egotists. Now they were propelled entirely by stock market traders. Children of the liquidity whirlpool, pretending to be Adam Smith's people, interested solely in cash values, not complex operating organizations of human beings performing in the most fundamental interests of society. Maybe that will be remembered as the turning point.

Well, the arb-raider was fine, but unfortunately it required at least an arb to be the point man. There are more of them than there are raider CEOs, but the supply is still limited, as is the junk financing. Wouldn't it be wonderful if the raider could be dispensed with entirely? Such a feat of technology. That's what you have in the recent voluntary restructurings, where the large company buys back stock with new debt. Where with the investment banker working the inside, the anonymous arbs working the outside, large corporations are persuaded to restructure themselves, to "enhance shareholder values", because it "appears" there "might" be a raid. "The arbs appear to be accumulating." It's Valhalla for the takeover crowd. If managements won't wake up to it, you wonder when the tax committees in Congress will.

Shall we quit?

Lawrence: Yes. You're a canny debater but we aren't getting anywhere. You may be right on a wealth of detail, but you're wrong on the big picture. I'll admit, though, you are saying a few things I haven't heard before. I think I can do a better job of it making the strong case in favor of hostile tender offers. Once we get into the golden parachutes and the greenmail this will all start to come together.

Michael: We'll continue tomorrow.

THE THIRD DAY

Lawrence: Your problem is you are challenging self-evident principles of economics and finance and human nature and common sense. You're wrong way Corrigan. You might as well argue there is no circle. Ask anyone in the Congress, for example, and he'll nod agreement that we have to be vigilant against the corporate manager's self-dealing and sloth. That's a fact of life, my friend. Open your eyes.

Michael: No, it's a common slur, not a fact. It is remarkable when you think about it that big business has thrived so far, notwithstanding the common antipathy for the people who run it. Just as the governments, Federal and State, go steadily along, propelled by legions of fine career civil servants, many of them highly skilled individuals who could earn much more in private industry, when right along side their efforts there exists the conventional, man in the street slur that they are all lazy bureaucrats feeding off the public dole. Just like our career people, men and women, in the armed services perform so well, give such dedicated service to our country, laboring mostly without any public awareness, and all the time being looked down on by a signficiant proportion of the general populace because they are military. The same with police. The same with politicians. What annoys me is that alone among the various unfairly thought of groups in society, you folks in the takeover crowd have developed a way to make fabulous fortunes orchestrating the bashing on businessmen. It's wrong. The profiting from this activity. Ralph Nader and Mark Green did it not to profit from it but because they believed in it. You do it to make money. And now you're going too far. You are breaking bones.

Lawrence: Ralph Nader and his "raiders" criticized business to get improved productivity because they knew the potential was there but ignored by lazy managers. We criticize inefficient management for the same reason --to get improved profitability because we know the potential is there, but ignored.

The thing that has probably given American management the worst black eye is the "golden parachutes". More than a third of the 250 largest industrial companies signing all those executives up to extravagant windfall compensation payments in the event a change in control happens. Every member of the Congress, every editorial writer, it seems, has condemned this spectacle of selfishness. Nothing business could have done would have confirmed its low standing more than these shoddy contracts have. They are something you cannot possibly justify. They refute all your notions about managers of public companies being upright people. The golden parachutes are a scandal.

Michael: Who invented the golden parachutes? Who first persuaded companies to put them in place?

Lawrence: Who knows? Who cares? They did it. No one made them adopt these things. You would have everyone believe that all these executives are so hard working, so dedicated to their company's mission, so altruistic. You put them in a class just below saints.

Michael: I do not.

Lawrence: But the golden parachutes tell the real story. If the company is under attack, what do the senior executives care about first? The company? The employees? The pensioners? The plant communities? The customers? Society? None of the above. They care about themselves. They indelicately go for the cash, as much as they can stuff in their pockets on the way out the door.

Some of these people have awarded themselves such lucrative golden parachutes that they probably hope a raider will appear. They won't want to hear you saying your stuff. No help wanted. Let the raiders come. We're ready for them. They're spiders waiting for flies.

The pervasive aroma of the golden parachutes proves my case against managers and in favor of takeovers. The prosecution rests.

Michael: The takeover law firms led the way with these arrangements. I agree with you. They are awful for business' image. Executives are entitled to reasonable salary continuation arrangements. Assurances against arbitrary or malicious action by a new control. Those are deserved and I support that. And like anyone else they are entitled to their deferred compensation and the profits on their stock and stock options. You don't call any of those things golden parachutes?

Lawrence: No.

Michael: But they are not entitled to fantastic, windfall salary and termination payments far exceeding what they would have earned in the normal course without a takeover, just because some entity acquires a control percentage or the whole company. You won't get an argument from me about those.

Lawrence: Wonderful. At last we are making

99

progress. You just threw out the baby. Why do you care who invented these things anyway? It's who agrees to take them that matters, not who suggested them. Adam and Eve ate the apple.

Michael: Because I've explained my main concern with hostile takeovers. That public company managements will be turned to pure self interest as a result of them. Symbolically it is notable that the takeover attorneys have been actively encouraging exactly this attitude from the start. Before golden parachutes were common, one of them was quoted in Fortune to the effect that "Investment bankers and us takeover lawyers make big fees in takeovers; why shouldn't executives?" What a horrible, primitive sense of values. That's an example of how takeovers pollute public companies. Takeovers don't discipline management. Nor do they motivate management. They corrupt management.

Lawrence: Hold it. You make it sound like some leading takeover lawyer waves his hand and all American managers have themselves golden parachutes. Even if the takeover lawyers suggested it, why didn't management say "No thank you. That would be self-centered for me to do that. I won't follow that advice."

Michael: You must understand how this began. More and more large companies started to turn to newly prominent takeover lawyers for defensive advice. "How do we keep the company independent?" That was their only question. They would not have consulted them unless they were given to believe from the press and the investment banking referrals that there was something the lawyers could do to defend target companies. All the major investment bankers had their favorite takeover lawyer they

100

would recommend to clients. The lawyers said that one of the first things the clients should do is give themselves golden parachutes. These are businessmen who know nothing about takeovers listening to legal experts. How the existence of the parachutes would deter a raider was probably left a little vague by the attorneys. There were suggestions for outside directors that it would help management think more clearly under fire, knowing they had this financial protection. And that everyone else was doing it. They made it sound like fitness training.

If you go to a doctor and he says you must take a long vacation, you don't say "No. That would be selfish of me." That's how these parachutes began. You research it someday. You'll see I'm right. They began with the takeover bar. The same lawyers who would later join the investment bankers in spreading the idea that if a takeover happens management, inside directors, should be still. They have a conflict of interest. Let the outside directors run the show. The trusting outside directors, the takeover lawyers and the investment bankers. Boy, what a combination!

People don't understand that the takeover crowd in New York wants to see executives have compensation deals that produce big personal windfalls from a hostile takeover. It's an out and out bribe attempt to get the managements not to try to avoid an auction, and instead achieve an even better transaction for Wall Street interests. And as a bonus for the takeover crowd, it gives business a worse reputation. Executives don't understand this, what's really going on. Most of them are embarrassed by these arrangements. For good reason. They contradict a new attitude toward pecuniary compensation that has been evolving in the widely held large scale organizations.

If outsiders are thinking of raiding the company, they read about these contracts in the SEC filings and they see that this is a company where maybe a takeover will have a little touch of Christmas morning in it. When the heat is on, the executives thus compromised will not be the "down in flames" types. That's good. That's important when the boys from Wall Street are in later during an actual takeover trying to get the company to opt for the auction instead of pursuing defensive strategies like antitrust or repurchase of the raider's shares, strategies that might keep the company independent. The executives have been put on an incentive plan like the investment bankers and the lawyers.

At bottom, takeovers have to do with a debasement of values one encounters in public companies. Most tactics which originate with the takeover crowd have that result.

Lawrence: Speaking of lower values, I'm reminded of the companies that pay "greenmail." Next to golden parachutes, greenmail is the management practice in the takeover area that has drawn the most criticism. Corporate officials protect themselves from ouster by paying a special profit to one aggressive shareholder to buy back his shares, usually a substantial block. Then the stock price falls out of bed when the purchase is publicly announced. This is repugnant to all observers. You can't find anyone who defends it.

Michael: "Greenmail" is a pejorative label which the takeover crowd coined as a catchy phrase for the press, to put companies that do it on the defensive.

Lawrence: Get to the point.

Michael: Within limits, I approve of companies using corporate funds to ensure the corporation's continued independence. I trust most boards of directors that if the price were too high, that if it was more suitable to see the company acquired, or at least dominated by a large holder, that they would acquiesce in that. But you can see that from my perspective there is something fine about public companies trying to live as they are, struggle for their own survival. That instinct of self preservation is what makes them so important. You can't just snuff that out whenever you like. You're correct. The market price drops on the announcement of a share repurchase, but usually not much below where it used to trade on the company's own prospects as an independent entity. Speculators sensing a takeover may lose money on their recent stock accumulation, but long term shareholders usually don't. They frequently benefit in time. There are examples of companies that have bought stock back from predators several times, and consistently gone on to greater prosperity, and much higher stock prices. There is nothing wrong with buying back stock. The general reflexive contempt for it speaks volumes about basic attitudes toward businessmen that are brilliantly exploited by the takeover crowd.

Lawrence: Nothing wrong with corporate servants applying the shareholder's money to a bribe that keeps them in office?

Michael: Applying the corporate money to a share purchase that keeps the company independent.

Forget your labels and address the substance of the thing.

Lawrence: You have a thin skin for some things, but a high tolerance for others, I'll say that. Greenmail is despicable.   The shareholders own the money that is used. You don't dispute that?

Michael: The corporation owns it.   The shareholders possess some of the classical indicia of ownership of the corporation, but by no means all. They don't have the management responsibility, the reality, the familiarity that involves.   They've probably even diversified their risk of a share price decline throughout a portfolio of other investments.

Lawrence: Management spends the money to bribe a raider into going away so management can stay in office.

Michael: Management causes the company to purchase the shares so the company can stay independent.   For the good of the entity, the institution.

Lawrence: That's criminal. It's stealing for heavens sakes. How dare a mere caretaker use other peoples' property like that.   He should be fired immediately. No hearing. Anything like that should require the prior approval of the shareholders. If management can make a case that it is good for the company then the shareholders will approve it at a stockholders meeting. Don't hide it. Get the skunk up on the table.

Michael: I've thought for years now that that there is a legalized form of market manipulation here. Buy a block of a company that looks like it will fight, announce it, then try to put them "in play" in a bidding contest. For a fall-back you can sell the block to them at a profit if the auction doesn't develop. People will be there to profit any way the system allows. I'd like to change that system, by making takeovers more difficult. That would eliminate the need to do the buybacks. Greenmail isn't the problem. Takeovers are the problem.

What you call greenmail is usually a legitimate act of self-help against the abuse of takeovers. Managements do it for only one reason. To preserve the company. If they don't do it one thing will lead to another and the company will likely be auctioned off to the highest bidder. You can't stand still in these situations. Big blocks seldom become little blocks.

And you're being inconsistent today. The raider who ends up a greenmailer would have preferred to have management look instead to their compensation arrangements and call in the bankers to hold an auction. As we discussed two days ago, greenmailers always make less money selling the shares back than they would if there were an all out bidding contest for the company. If your theory about the motives behind golden parachutes were true, managements would go for the takeover alternative and the compensation, instead of buying out the predator and then facing a blizzard of shareholder lawsuits accusing them of waste of corporate assets. You haven't thought it through.

One cannot condemn greenmail until it is first concluded that takeovers are beneficial. To oppose greenmail is to favor hostile takeovers. There is no middle ground there. What the takeover crowd has had Congress considering, and this is typical, is legislation to forbid companies from buying their stock back from raiders. Securities firms even got the legislature of New York to enact a statute to that effect. You might as well pass laws saying "whoever has a new five percent shareholder must be sold to the highest bidder".

So it's obvious why the takeover crowd dislikes greenmail. It aborts the bidding contests. It takes fees out of the mouths of the investment bankers. Nearly all of them are more interested in the merger fees than in the clients remaining independent. It also cuts into the more lucrative performances of the takeover lawyers. And the arbs, it hurts the arbs the most of of all. They have a double disaster. Not only do they miss out on profits from a bidding contest. They run a risk of losing money on the stock they already own.

In the takeover crowd's code of conduct, greenmail is the high treason. The press has been sympathetic to their campaign against the practice. And one of the nimble takeover investment bankers even came up with the incredible idea to amend the public company's charter so that it would be forbidden to pay greenmail. More than a dozen companies went along and adopted such a provision. How's that for unilateral disarmament before the takeover machine? In all of this propaganda about greenmail, no one speaks up for the result that another public company has endured a threat to its existence. I'll champion that cause any day. It's a fine outcome if the price is at all practical.

Lawrence: You mischaracterized that fellow's charter amendment idea. It's purpose is to deter the raider from the outset, to let him know that he won't be able to engage in your legalized form of stock manipulation. So he won't buy the stock to begin with.

Michael: That reasoning is so flawed one has to suspect the wish that gave birth to the thought. You don't deter raiders by eliminating their fall-back position. Indeed, raiders usually vote <u>for</u> the anti-greenmail clause. You have to address their preferred result — putting the target in play. Repurchasing the shares is one of the few ways to take a company out of play.

Lawrence: The charter amendment you refer to doesn't prohibit greenmail. It just says shareholders have to vote on it. So it takes longer. And is more open for all to consider before it happens.

That bring us to the odious subject of poison pills. There an arrogant management implements a grotesque legal gimmick which is intended to make the company virtually impossible to take over. It is a dividend of paper that purports to give the target company's shareholders a right to buy the <u>raider's</u> own common stock at 50% off the market price, as a penalty, if any raider acquires a certain percentage of the target and then tries to finish an all out acquisition of the target. The raider would have to commit waste to do the merger of the two. Sell its own shares at one-half off their value. These pills are another outrage brought to us by your revered American managers. Poison pills are revolting. Managements that adopt them are disloyal. People like you who defend them should be ashamed.

Michael: You didn't hear me defend them. They are wrong because they are deliberately designed to harm the corporation and shareholders. But there is bad news and good news in poision pills.

Lawrence: I knew you'd see something good in them.

Michael: The bad news is that taken at face value they are indeed an affront to shareholders, and another black eye for management. The worst black eye. If you are disgusted with them, imagine how I feel. How would you like to have authored the original "fair price" clause, designed it for submission to shareholders for their prior approval, and then see high steppers in the takeover crowd eight years later use your basic idea, even the same wording in places, fashion a stone age version of it and advise their clients to adopt it by board action alone --no vote of shareholders? That's the poison pill.

Lawrence: I don't believe my ears. You said rights of shareholders. You don't care about shareholders.

Michael: They have fundamental rights which must still be respected under current state corporate laws and the judicial theory of the corporation. Much as I would like to see a change in the ability of outsiders to force sales of public companies, there are rules concerning shareholder rights that must be observed until changed legitimately. A board has no right to institute basic structural changes in the legal relationship of the shareholders to the corporation without a shareholders vote. That's what the poison pill purports to do.

Lawrence: The courts should be rejecting these things out of hand. Instead they are sanctioning the adoption of them before a takeover, with a warning that they must be used responsibly. By definition a poison pill is irresponsible, for the reason you stated. It by-passes shareholders.

What's the good news?

Michael: Maybe it's poetic justice that the poison pills don't work. The draftsmanship in most of them is lacking. And even if they were expertly drafted, were I a raider I could turn the poison pill back on the target company, use it to isolate the target from all possible white knights and to stampede the directors, and then get control at a bargin price. Maybe you and the fund managers should hush up about poison pills. They are actually the takeover crowd's trojan horse.

Lawrence: If that's so, the Trojans forgot to get inside.

Michael: Look how prevalent they are. Do you think that would have happened, with all the takeover experts participating in it, if they worked? There have already been sad examples. Companies that have poison pills would be well advised to redeem them, cancel them voluntarily, instead of waiting for someone who understands the technology to pop out and ensnare them. CEOs who have swallowed them fail to understand the takeover jungle. It's amusing to see the number of high priced lawyers now who admit to being specialists in poison pills. It's like being an authority on the graffiti on subway cars.

Trust me, they don't work. They're worse than nothing.

Lawrence: But obviously managements adopt them believing they do work. That's the indictment of management. Their motives are the lowest. If the pills worked, then as you say they'd be an affront. Another example of management arrogating the law to themselves. Golden parachutes, greenmail and now poison pills. Tip your king over Mac.

Michael: I don't blame the rash of poison pills on American management either. Managers have been gulled into adopting them, just like the excessive golden parachutes. Once again the takeover lawyers and investment bankers are the ones entirely responsible, and the courts are starting to throw the book at their clients, just like a few courts have been outraged at the parachutes.

I don't find it unforgivable that American management has put its faith in large takeover law firms. Managers are trained to listen to lawyers. It's awful when they don't. I've seen it. These takeover law firms have been eulogized by the financial press as the best in the business and recommended highly by prominent investment banking firms. Management naturally hires them and trusts them, especially because this is an arcane field. I fault management for its gullibility, and not doing its homework on this area, but not for its venality.

Lawrence: So your alibi is: Anything improper that managers do is the fault of the takeover lawyers. It's too pat.

Michael: It's true here. You takeover mavens have done an award winning job of promoting to the press that certain lawyers are head and shoulders over all the rest. "No one else is fit to shine their shoes." You succeeded. American management now listens to these advisors that you selected. If you did not have the takeover bar, you would not have golden parachutes. You would not have poison pills. End of discussion.

110

Lawrence: The takeover bar doesn't hold such sway over business executives. You have them mesmerizing CEOs.

Michael: I have proof.

Lawrence: What?

Michael: The statistics I gave you yesterday.

Lawrence: Yes?

Michael: One company out of 55 surviving in good health over almost 10 years.

Lawrence: So?

Michael: It takes powerfully influential doctors to stay in the operating room with a failure rate like that.

Lawrence: Then why have we had greenmail? You say the takeover crowd opposes stock buybacks.

Michael: That's the single exception in this field, where most managements can add 2 and 2 by themselves. They can see the definitive advantage in separating the raider from his block of stock. And because of their faith in the company they can see the financial benefits to remaining shareholders. But a number of prominent target companies have still been skillfully distracted from that approach by the takeover advisors.

Lawrence: You oversimplify. Now that we have laid the groundplan of the skull-duggery of American managers, the lengths they will go to to watch out for themselves, I want to come back to the fundamental justifications for hostile takeovers. Takeovers create wealth, and that is always good. There hasn't been a single so-called raid that didn't create significantly increased stock values.

Michael: You mean the raider goes into a secret room and says "Shazam" and the money he needs appears? You'd be well advised not to pursue that creation myth. The Mafia might create wealth, but takeovers don't.

Lawrence: It's no myth. Share prices of targets rise more than 30% on average, and share prices of bidders rise 4%. So it's not just a transfer of wealth.

Michael: Hostile cash takeovers extinguish equity. Once the equity is gone it's gone. They sneer at the whole purpose of trading markets, which is to attract nervous investment into capital assets. The only thing I see them creating is disproportionate riches for the raiders and the close knit takeover crowd of speculators and advisors. And yes, sporadically a shareholder might make an unexpected stock market profit. But there is not the kind of consistent, broadly available "wealth" that could ever commend takeovers as a national preference. They are harmful, not beneficial. The entrepreneurial takeovers today depend primarily upon new managers being willing to run the risks of greater debt. If that is what you mean by "creating wealth", we don't need it so much that we should tolerate an assault on the very concept of the public company.

Lawrence: Do you want me to total up the billions of profits, premiums over market, that we paid out in takeovers in the last ten years? That's not wealth? Don't the shareholders benefit because they sell out at a higher price, either into the market or in the offer?

Michael: You can't simply add that up and say "Q.E.D., takeovers are good." It's far more complex than that. The few shareholders who are in on the six or seven takeovers that occur in a year could be making something, and not all equally either, while the many who are investing elsewhere amid this raucous atmosphere, not to mention society, could be losing far more. We already discussed the costs of the takeover distraction to the thousands of companies not taken over. That's the worst part of it. The penalty this behavior extracts from normal operating business, which must adjust to these new standards. You can't measure that. But one day you can wake up and find your whole system has deteriorated. Another aspect of it is the losses to people who owned what they thought were high grade corporate bonds of a major company like Unocal or Phillips or Union Carbide, before the company "restructures" itself to avoid being a target of a raid.

Lawrence: A couple of points: First, individuals don't own junk bonds. Institutions — the big boys do. So no one who can't fend for themselves is hurt by . . .

Michael: I'm not talking about junk bonds. I'm talking about previously issued investment grade bonds that become junk when the takeover advisors get through restructuring the company in response to a takeover threat.

Lawrence: The lawyers should have guarded against that when they wrote the indentures setting out the terms of the bonds. They should have provided for an interest rate adjustment in the event the bonds ever became less than investment grade.

Michael: You mean the underwriting investment bankers. They're the ones who negotiate the terms on behalf of the public. Is that where we are headed Lawrence? Shall we start putting provisions in the indentures that protect against the consequences of management deliberately trying to cripple their company to avoid its becoming a takeover target? Has it come to that already? I know that's where we are headed, but I have hoped that it is still a ways off and that we can all cooperate to avoid it.

Lawrence: Everyone feels a need to attack junk bonds if they oppose takeovers.

Michael: The attack on junk bonds may be overdone. I don't know. It seems like some pretty sophisticated people price them and buy them when they're issued for takeovers. Perhaps they're legitimate, unless there is unclean money there. I gather authorities are watching to keep them from being too much in the hands of the widows and orphans, the pensioners and the S&Ls, and the policy holders reserves. People who attack hostile takeovers and junk bonds are chasing two rabbits. They are different questions. Whether junk bonds present a financial danger to our economy or not, hostile takeovers are still wrong and we should stop them.

Lawrence: It annoys me to hear some people predicting doom's day as a result of the levels of corporate debt. They don't know what they're talking about. It's like people in the 1920's being shocked at home mortgages. Debt levels in our corporate economy are still low compared to companies abroad.

Michael: But they have reserves we don't know about.

Lawrence: Still, we are not overextended, I mean our corporations. We are passing up capital that our trade competitors employ.

Michael: Whether we are or we are not, I don't think that's the issue in takeovers.

Lawrence: Inflation will probably pay off all the junk bonds. There's nothing wrong with business adjusting to new standards of debt/equity ratios either. As the late Senator Dirksen said, the only people who don't change are dead.

Next point. Because takeovers redirect assets to their highest use, over the long haul they promote efficiency and jobs. That's a good.

Michael: We already shot down the higher uses excuse. And don't you try to bring the miseries of involuntary unemployment into this conversation. Takeovers actually cost jobs. I won't rest a case against them on that ground, because operating independent companies themselves cut back on jobs for the good of the entire company. Hopefully, one day we will understand how to avoid ever having to do that. It is the leading challenge for business today. Hostile takeovers probably cost a greater percentage of headquarters jobs than workers' jobs. Hostile takeovers don't create any new jobs. That's the main thing. Except at investment banking and law firms. We don't need them to improve the employment picture in the U.S. The spokesmen for takeovers mislead people about this. Representatives of labor have studied it carefully and had their fill of hostile takeovers. They see employees traded and bartered as chattel.

Much of the corporate overhead a raider lops off at a large company in the first few weeks involves functions that give the public company its special character. By definition there are layers of management in all large public companies that are inherent in the group activity which is the essence of them, the substitute for the private entrepreneur. I think you will find that the civic, the social conscience areas of a company are particularly ravaged when the cost accountants land in the helicopters after a hostile takeover. Berlin blockade-like conditions are imposed while the acquisiton debt load is worked off. It's a much different company. It may be seen, with a wave of the economist's hand, as leaner with less unnecessary overhead, less fat. But it is also private, not public any more, and it does not have its former potential for society and that's not something we can sweep under the rug. This happens to some extent in voluntary LBOs too, but it isn't as severe because of the negotiated circumstances.

You and I could cut the tax burden in a lot of states and cities. But we could also drastically change the quality of those places.

Lawrence: Hostile takeovers also benefit society by increasing the Government's tax revenues. The companies are made more profitable in the long run. . .

Michael: How long? When the interest deductions run out?

Lawrence: . . . and that increases taxes, as do asset sales. In addition, when all those people sell their stock at a profit, they pay taxes on that profit.

And the junk bond lenders pay taxes on the interest.

Michael: Your last point won't hold up. We are talking about the large, prominent takeovers. A great proportion of the shares in the large companies are held by tax exempt entities, primarily pension plans. Some prominent institutional money managers deal only with tax exempt clients. And you can't be sure the purchasers of the junk bonds are taxpayers either. So it's unsafe to generalize.

Lawrence: But that fund money gets recycled to retirees, who spend it and generate further economic activity and tax revenue.

Michael: The retirees would get their same benefits even if we had never heard of takeovers. It is not helping retirees.

Lawrence: You made the incredible comment the other day that shareholders of a widely held company merely facilitate each other's liquidity, and don't contribute much to the enterprise.

Michael: Professor Berle said that.

Lawrence: Aren't you whittling away at shareholders' rights?

Michael: It's not revolutionary, not any more. It's theory adapting to fact. Take a public company that does not do equity financing. It generates all its capital from within, or from debt that is repaid from profits. A lot of large companies are like that, a majority of them. Berle asked: What do shareholders contribute? Nothing. He saw them as temporary participants in a stream of earnings from the company. They get dividends. And they cooperate to make each others' holdings liquid. They meet in the market. But none of that affects the typical company -- except for the worth of officer stock options and other employee stock plans. A single healthy company with a sound balance sheet could theoretically see its stock go to zero and it shouldn't affect the operations of the company. I don't want to carry this too far. The shareholders occupy an important place in the series of events that is the public company. Economically and legally the role of the shareholder is still crucial. My point is, we should not elevate the new class of public company shareholders above the importance of the public company itself. Unquestionably, when it comes to being forced into sale by mere record holders who don't have a shred of an ownership interest, the public company ought to be sovereign now, in my opinion. The term "shareholders" should no longer be indiscriminately used in the same sense as when a company was privately owned by a small group of individuals.

Lawrence: That's Marxist -- the "state" is greater than the people who "created" it. It's contrary to our culture and principles.

Michael: The modern public company which is totally owned by no one, no class, certainly not the state, and which, depending solely on intelligence and energy, is open to being directed in the next generation by the children of its factory workers. That's something remarkable that Karl Marx didn't foresee. Public capitalism is slowly fulfilling the nightmare Marx dreaded: a bourgeoisie without a proletariat. And something else he couldn't have imagined: Classical ownership of the means of production quietly passing out of shareholders' hands, but not into the hands of any state or central authority.

Lawrence: What do you mean by no one totally owns the public company?

Michael: No one has both legal ownership of the share interests and responsibility for the day to day operations.

Lawrence: Like the Russian Government's view of the populace, you have a low opinion of shareholders indeed. Abolition of private property.

Michael: Do you mean shareholders that own the stock?

Lawrence: I mean shareholders. What do you mean? What is this nonsense?

Michael: You know. People like me that really own it, or institutions that get to vote it because they are hired for a percentage fee to manage a fund that owns it? Which do you mean?

Lawrence: There's no difference.

Michael: Wrong. I have always had deep regard for individual shareholders. They are a wonderful group. It is sad that they have been drowned out. They are invariably patient, loyal, supportive of corporate management. If a hostile takeover is made at a substantial premium over market, a great proportion of the individual shareholders will not want to sell. I can't say enough about them. I wish all shareholders were individuals. Continued growth in IRAs could have helped that. You don't have to explain the changed circumstances of the modern public company to individual shareholders. They understand it instinctively. They are sensitive to their lessened role, in return for which they have liquidity and diversification, and they always show respect for the public company and for its management, unless management has really fouled up. And then they vote for insurgents if there's a proxy fight, but they still respect the company. Sophisticates call them dupes for going along with management, sheep. I don't think so. Individual shareholders, the vast majority of them, are civilized. They have wisdom and real class.

Lawrence: And the funds are uncivilized . . .

Michael: I could think of stronger terms for some of them.

Lawrence: Because they are trying to improve the retirement benefits, for example, for their consitutents?

Michael: Please stop saying that. Improved fund performance does not increase pension benefits. It just reduces a sponsor's annual pension expense. The funds don't care about retirement benefits. They only care about getting fees, and more money to manage for fees. It's a mockery that they _are_ the stock market today, yet most of them can't even perform as well as the S&P 500. So they are frantic for takeovers to cover up their inadequacies. Some fund managers in the last few years have given the name "shareholder" a bad connotation.

Lawrence: These people are fiduciaries. Most of them have duties to plan participants under ERISA, the employees retirement income security act passed by the Congress. You are familiar with trustees, the law of fiduciary duties. That's what

120

they are, fiduciaries. They have to get the best price for the plan participants. That's why they do what they do.

Michael: If we have managers of tens of billions of pension monies in our country rooting for hostile takeovers because that is their duty, then whatever law imposes such a duty ought to be reexamined. Things are backwards. The real parties in interest in those pension plans are American workers. Takeovers work a terrible tragedy on the people involved. It's a travesty to finance them in the name of wage earners and retired people.

Lawrence: But that may be in their best interests.

Michael: Says who? You remind me of a recent incident in which the Department of Labor and a Federal judge in New York both made a shambles of how our system achieves the supposed best interest of workers under the ERISA law. A company that became a takeover target had already sold 20% of its shares to an employee stock ownership plan, taking back a long term note. The chief executive, the trustee of the plan, set up secret ballots at all the plants and canvassed the participating white collar employees to see if they wanted the shares in the plan to be tendered. They voted overwhelmingly, more than 9-to-1, against tendering. You'd think the government agency and the court would approve that election mechanism. Not so. The Department of Labor and the court both wanted some complete outsider, or some financial insitution, to take custody of the stock and decide on its own whether to tender the stock. Don't listen to the employees. The Federal judge went out of his way to scold the company for harboring any ideas that the desire of the participant employees was binding. He said he was looking out for future participants. It was pointed out to the judge that if the stock were to be tendered to the raider the plan would end and those present salaried employees would get all of the profit proceeds. Why then should their preference against tendering not be conclusive? He would hear none of it.

This is disturbing. Talk about separating management and ownership of large enterprises. How would you like to see the authorities separate you from the decision to hold or sell your securities, especially when they are securities of your employer and a takeover is involved. Even though there is a mortgage on them, you should still be entitled to vote to sell and enjoy the benefit of any profit once the mortgage has been paid. That's what was going on there. Just because there was an ERISA plan involved, the Federal court and the Federal Government both felt they had the right to shunt the uninformed employees off to one side, and appoint strangers who would decide what was best for them. It was an example of terrible judgement on the part of the court and the Department of Labor. But that's the kind of system we could be slowly moving to. The wealth will get detached from its owners, and some central authority will decide how it is to be invested. That's a lot more serious than management of corporations being detached.

Lawrence: I'm not interested in this story. I don't know the background, except to say that Federal courts don't act arbitrarily. Maybe the court there was concerned that the management was coercing the employees in the voting. There are secret ballots and there are secret ballots.

Michael: That wasn't the problem. The company would have let the judge conduct the ballot. That wouldn't have changed his mind. Federal judges are only human. That is just an object lesson that shows we have lost our direction with these fiduciary concepts. Throughout our discussion I have been concentrating on the desirability of stopping the takeover bids. Perhaps that's only necessary because we have moved out of the era of individual stock ownership, to the era of pooled accounts. There are some strange notions around about what that means.

Lawrence: You're a cry baby. You want the giant public companies, with all the good things they can do for society. But you don't want to be bothered by the other side of that, the giant pension plans, and the institutions that we need to manage them. It is really the rebirth of stockholder control over a no account management.

Michael: There's nothing objectionable in giant pension funds. They're fine, except maybe the investment management function might be spread out more. I just wouldn't let them vote on takeovers to the same extent as I would the individual shareowner, that's all. The large companies are public now. They should stay that way. And if they are ever going to return to control by interests outside management, it certainly shouldn't be fund managers who have no ownership stake in the shares.

Lawrence: I was thinking last night, I wonder who rules these fund managers you loathe? Who motivates them to this myopic quest for stock market profits?

Michael: I don't loathe them. I think they are fixated on profits now, market profits now.

Lawrence: Answer the question.

Michael: I know. I have a problem.

Lawrence: You sure do. It's the treasurers in the large public companies that lay down the law to those pension funds. They tell them "Look, here's a portion of my portfolio. I've given portions to four other guys. The four who do the best over the next year, they stay. The fifth, he goes." What do you expect the fund managers to do when your esteemed corporate America is telling them those are the marching orders? One could step back and say that the "takeover crowd," as you call it, has created for fund managers an opportunity to perform up to the expectations of your corporate bureaucracy.

Michael: You're right. We are too heavily dependent now on defined benefit pension plans. These encourage companies to flog their fund managers into better portfolio performance. The better the fund performs, the less the annual contribution the company has to make, and the better the company's reported earnings. It's a vicious circle. The only explanation I can offer is that the managements of the large public companies as a group are not yet sufficiently aware of their part in the problem and of their ability to perhaps act on it. A good case can be made that portfolio performance resulting from takeover profits is not the kind of excellence that corporate treasurers should be looking for, or reward. It's too volatile. And if it's consistent, those profits could carry substantial hidden liabilities some day. They certainly are not a result of skilled prudent investment. You identified a sore spot, no question. I have hoped that public company managements will rethink their inadvertent role in all of this. They seldom talk to each other about takeovers. It's too intimate. They definitely are a part of the problem, but it's tunnel vision. It's not a double standard.

Lawrence: What are you going to do to change it? Managements will be sued if they don't pick the best fund managers.

Michael: The problem is a surfeit of these linear fiduciary ideas we still have with us, ideas developed in a different society. Centuries ago the English had to create courts of Equity because their courts of Law were so rigidly logical that they were arriving at unwise results. In today's context I don't think it is right or required that a corporate management must choose the most successful fund managers, regardless of profound questions for society raised by how they earn their portfolio profits. The college students have made that point with their South African disinvestment campaigns. I believe large companies collectively can draw a line around funds that get too involved in takeovers. And voters should do the same to elected officials that manage public pension moneys as if they were arbitrageurs.

But let's not lose sight of the first point in all of this. Funds did not create the takeover environment. Corporate treasurers certainly didn't. The takeover crowd did. Then they wink at an ever-widening audience and say, "Come on. Join in. It's great. You'll do better than you ever did." But it's not great. It's an excess that needs checking.

Lawrence: I see it just the opposite. It is symmetrical. The presence of the large worker pension funds as shareholders serves to enhance the threat of a takeover, which keeps management on its toes. What justice! Blue collar savings cracking the whip over the stuffed shirt managers. Ah capitalism!

Michael: We should have stopped yesterday. You're back to reciting the same trite phrases. For the third time, takeovers don't motivate management at all. Not only is the constant threat of a takeover a counter-productive distraction, there is no end to the ways in which it can disrupt the orderly growth of a public company. Here's another factor that should trouble us: Why should young business and engineering and law school graduates pin career hopes on a position with a firm of a size or type that is more likely to be a vulnerable takeover target? Who wants to throw in with a company that will be owned by a raider some day, maybe just when you're working your way to a senior position? The message there for the new recruits is to stay away from public companies or else seek out the giant firms — the Exxons and the IBMs and the R.J.R. Nabiscos because they are less vulnerable. Better yet, go with merger departments of large investment banking firms. Avoid deserving companies. That's the kind of adverse trend that no one notices until the damage is long done. We want to encourage our best young men and women to go with the smaller and medium size public companies. This takeover surge is subverting that, I'm sure of it. It has to. That is why we need responsible politicians to get into this. It is a dangerous subject for them but also a vital one. The country is hurting, while the Federal Government seems to be cheering it on.

Lawrence: If young people are good, they'll survive a takeover. They'll land on their feet. If they're not good, then that proves they shouldn't have been in that position in the first place -- too much fat. The young people don't have an unalienable right to a job with a company free from takeovers.

Michael: You are missing the whole point. The young people have their expectations. We are dealing with the most basic human motivations, the kind of thing any society is dependent on, even primitive societies. Whenever you are talking about values you must take the conditions you favor and extend them to all the possible situations, here all public companies, and then see what you have created. You persistently hide from this Kantian imperative.

Lawrence: Young people don't have that much to worry about. Usually only the thin layer at the top is affected by takeovers, the ones who brought the enterprise to a standstill. It helps the rest because it gives the company a new thrust forward.

Michael: Takeovers also interfere with the thoroughness of planning. They have to have that effect. I don't want to fall into your short term, long term trap. But you know very well takeovers mean market value. Now. Today's market value. It is more difficult to concentrate on intricate long range business analysis, which is not all financial, when you have that kind of noise in your ears day after day. As technology grows more complex, the lead time from identification of new markets to production of the new products for those markets gets longer and longer. This is a primary reason for the growth of the large public company. It is corrupting to have the hedonist carpe diem takeover attitude distort that process.

Also, the constant threat of the arbitrary takeover bid bores beneath all employee morale in the large public company. It encourages employees to think of themselves first, the company last. Because if there is a hostile takeover, that's very likely the way they will be treated. It affects productivity, team play, trust, commitment.

Lawrence: And that's very likely the way they'll be treated by their own management without a takeover bid, too. Nothing like those pre-Christmas time mass layoffs to swell employees' hearts with sympathy for those unhappy senior executives and directors, and their poor families.

Michael: Management determined layoffs are different than hostile takeover determined layoffs. Employees understand that, I believe.

Lawrence: Are you serious?

Michael: You're the fellow that was bemoaning fat in companies and the reluctance of management to take economy measures. You have no right to criticize management over layoffs.

Lawrence: Nor do you have a right to criticize takeovers over fear of layoffs. It's obvious that to the laid-off employee, it makes no difference what prompted the layoff. Let's switch the subject.

A recent study showed that a surprising percentage of Fortune 500 CEOs either didn't own any stock in their firms or owned less than $100,000 worth. If those overpaid people won't even risk that money in their own companies, that tells you a lot about their attitude toward the enterprise. They don't think like stockholders. Stock ownership is the litmus test of corporate loyalty.

Michael: Generals don't own stock in their armies, at least we hope not.

Lawrence: Oh for heavens sake.

Michael: University professors don't own stock in the schools. We are talking about a similar class of professionals — the career business executives who run modern corporations. The main thing that motivates them is not the money. It is their reputation, together with the institution that shapes them. This latter phenomenon was as alien to Adam Smith as radio was to Sir Isaac Newton. Physics is fully in the 20th century but a noisey part of economics is still in the 18th. I think top managers could function well without any financial investment in their firms, stock or otherwise. We don't want public company managers who are motivated primarily by personal wealth. They might run the company for the compensation plans. In mounting their raids some corporate Napoleons have a keen eye on the larger personal compensation that comes with a larger company. We shouldn't motivate managers to engage in such empire building. Or managers might be tempted to self dealing so subtle that the accountants and the disclosure rules wouldn't catch it. Nor do we want today's managers thinking like stockholders. The altered expectations and motivations of today's managers is crucial to the quite enormous development from private enterprise to corporate enterprise.

There are beneficial cultural influences within the large public company now that actually deemphasize the individual pursuit of wealth. And without question a management must now take into account more factors than present stockholders' already detached and highly diversified interests. On the contrary, management now shoulders a responsibility for the business enterprise that stockholders have left behind. It is the managers who think most like owners because their responsibility is getting to be more of a piece with classical ownership than the increasingly depersonalized dominion over the shares. If we had management currently thinking only of that class of people who own the bare tokens, the shares alone, among many other investments, we could have economic chaos. Which is perhaps what you want, because you think with your wits you'll come out better than your neighbor.

Some of these executive surveys are also imperfect. Most CEOs have a huge personal financial stake tied up in their own companies. They have ERISA pensions. They have supplemental pensions. They have deferred compensation already earned but not paid to them for tax saving reasons. They have stock options and savings plan contributions. In most cases you'll probably find that the bulk of the CEO's estate is tied up in his company. Maybe not in the stock, where he is dependent each day on the market price. And it's not liquid either. So it's ridiculous to say he has no stake in the company, even if that is appropriate and I'm not sure that it is to get best performance from a person in our fundamentally new system. Executives and directors not owning stock has been overdone. It's a vestige of the obsolete ideas of private corporate ownership. We are in a new world with these large companies.

On occasion I have wondered about the idea of some kind of incentive keyed to book value, not market price, whereby a CEO would have a reward for good performance but at the same time it would be an incentive for him to step aside if performance is poor. For example, instead of a stock option there might be a contract to buy special stock according to a formula that assumes a rising book value. If things go the wrong way, he is relieved of his obligation but only if he steps down well in advance, not at the very end. The longer he waits the more he is committed personally. It might be useful. State law might provide for this in lieu of continuing to let the institutions vote stock they don't own. Or as a part of staggering the right to vote so it takes account of the period of ownership. But I'm leery of fiddling with a system that has operated so well. It deserves a great deal more thought.

Lawrence: Suppose we had a law or a social compact or whatever you want that prohibited all unilateral takeovers. "Hostile" takeovers as you call them. The only deals that could be done would be ones where target management endorsed them. Voluntarily agreed to support a merger, because of the price or other factors.

Michael: That's essentially the way it was until this takeover epidemic of recent years. It didn't require a law. Businessmen and lenders and investment bankers and lawyers and the rest respected one another. We need to revive that spirit.

Lawrence: Okay. Let's say a reformed raider comes to the CEO. Now he has to use carrots. No more sticks. He manages to get a meeting and he says "I'll pay twice the market price for all your shares. Cash. Please recommend the deal to your shareholders and we'll close it in 45 days." What's next? Does management have to go along? Under your system, do they have a legal duty to?

Michael: No.

Lawrence: What if he proposes to pay three times the market price?

Michael: No, not necessarily.

Lawrence: What if he proposes to pay ten times the market price?

Michael: Management would take it, I'm pretty sure.

Lawrence: But what if they don't?

Michael: They'd be sued if news of what they did became public, and the courts might say they went to an extreme. They might not. Courts would be more conscious of the role of widely held public companies in society, of the importance of protecting them in their day to day functions against the disincentives of takeovers.

Lawrence: You see what I'm driving at don't you?

Michael: Yes.

Lawrence: You don't want takeovers to be controlled by outside influences.

Michael: By outside buyers or speculators. That's correct.

Lawrence: Just by internal influences.

Michael: Right. I don't object to spontaneous mergers, where companies yield their independence because managements decide on their own it's a good idea.

Lawrence: Well all I've done is try to get a little spontaneity going that's all. My ferocious raider is now a pussy cat. He's asking "please." He has no power to go over managements' heads. We are in your Camelot. No one makes hostile offers any more. They are frowned on. The point is this: If management can initiate offers that you don't object to . . .

Michael: Right.

Lawrence: . . . why can't they be put in a position of responding to outside offers?

Michael: They can. You can't stop talk.

Lawrence: But do they have any obligations, any legal duties then?

Michael: Yes. They always have to act in the best interests of the corporation, including the shareholders, but not only the shareholders. That's the rule.

Lawrence: And in my situation how do we decide when they have fulfilled such an amorphous obligation?

Michael: In a great many instances you won't have to. Management will say "Yes" when the price is right, and the buyer will make it right if he wants the company enough. If the price rejected is too low plaintiffs attorneys won't want to incur the expense of a law suit because under my ideal system the bar will understand that the courts will require an egregious circumstance to impose liability. You will find though, that by changing the legal standard now in use by the courts, and also by placing the burden of proof on the challengers, the number of court cases will be manageable and, I think, readily decided.

Lawrence: If the price is right then management doesn't have your proper respect for the corporation. They're selling it down the river for filthy money. I thought you condemned that.

Michael: I told you the first day that I am reluctant to override a management decision to sell. We're just talking here about how that comes up.

Lawrence: But you wouldn't let courts force them to sell?

Michael: Yes, I would, in the extreme cases. An unusually heavy burden would be on the plaintiff though.

Lawrence: A burden to show what?

Michael: To show that the economic benefits of the deal to shareholders are so overwhelming, so exceptional, as to outweigh all other countervailing factors, including primarily the benefits to society of keeping this public company as well as all public companies generally free of the intimidation and distraction and disincentive that comes with the kind of takeover mentality we have today. In other words, only in the very rare case would management have a duty to sell. The price would have to be most unusual.

Lawrence: How can courts apply a test like that?

Michael: By taking one step at a time and sticking to the precise facts at hand. You'd be surprised how good the courts are at applying standards like that. They deal with them everyday. A body of case law builds up by accretion. The key is establishing the basic premise. That society and therefore the law leans strongly in favor of continuing public companies and against uninvited takeovers. Once we all agree on that, the system will work fine and shareholders will get their windfalls in the clearly deserving cases. Or else management may be held liable. Also don't forget that a management that is allowed by the law to say "No" has to live with a stock market price. It may be a far cry from the proposed acquisition price. That has an influence on managers. You'd be surprised how aware they can be of things like that. Give them a chance. And we still would have proxy contests to unseat poorly performing management.

In a regime such as I advocate, we would probably expect managements to disclose in advance their general attitude toward receiving such acquisition proposals. Some companies are more dependent on the equity markets than others. If they disclosed a closed mind attitude toward merger feelers, and their stock price behaved poorly and interfered with their financing and other capital plans, that wouldn't be lost on them.

But take the other case. Suppose a prosperous company made it clear that they would never, ever look kindly on an outside acquisition or break up proposal. And suppose their stock behaved very well despite that. Then isn't that the end of the whole issue? Why should any court step in to protect shareholders from something they have indicated they didn't care about? This thought experiment focuses attention on the dramatically different types of shareholders we now place all in the same boat. In some cases, today, courts are wrestling with the rights of regular shareholders who don't need and don't want the courts' interference. They aren't in the stock for a takeover windfall. Our legal system today lets 5 minute shareholders come in and assert all the rights of 5 year shareholders. That's absurd.

There might be advantages to a stock market in which investors could choose between companies that are cool to a merger and those that say they would entertain such things. Maybe this whole problem would solve itself.

People keep coming back to changing the law governing takeovers, and everyone assumes by that we mean the legislature changing the law. I believe that a thoughtful and far sighted opinion by a highly respected judge, or a respected panel of judges, might begin a process of truly constructive change. An opinion that confronts this persistent and outmoded concept of the modern shareholder's ownership rights. An opinion that courageously declares the community's overriding interests in these corporate control disputes. In fact, the judge-made law has been more influential in the development of our present corporation legal theory than the statutes have been. The trend in American corporation law has been for the state legislatures, which create the corporations, to gradually remove earlier statutory restrictions on corporate management. For example, what business the company can lawfully conduct, when new stock can be sold, for how much, whether and when warrants can be sold, when one class of stock can be treated differently than another, when certain dividends are payable. And so on. It has been the courts that have become the guardians of this shareholder as owner concept. The idea that managers are trustees for the shareholders. That the managers must use their ever broader authority under the statutes for the exclusive benefit of the shareholders. In almost all phases of day to day corporate activity these ideas will continue to be correct and essential. Only in the limited areas of induced acquisitions do the ideas need bold revision. I think judges are in a position now to open the windows a little and let fresh thinking into this. I hope they do it. Perhaps the courts need some further basic policy signal from the legislatures to even start the process. But it is the courts that will have the main burden of implementing a new approach. That's why we need the finest possible judges.

Lawrence: You really have gone around the bend with these ideas you have of publicly held companies and those who run them.

Michael: Publicly held for a long time. Include that.

Lawrence: Right. How long?

Michael: A generation. More. I don't know. It depends. A fairly long time. It's the antiquity that gains them a certain prejudice in their favor.

Lawrence: Let's say someone acquires all the stock of one of these historic landmarks of yours. It continues about its business. Employs the same people, mostly. Maybe has more debt and pays less taxes. There's nothing wrong with that. But it's still substantially the same factor in its markets and in the communities where it exists. What's different that's so important?

Michael: It is owned. It is no longer a self-responsible entity. That's the difference.

Lawrence: But <u>why</u> is that different?

Michael: Before you had an independent entity responsible to its own sense of its own mission. It had its own ways, its own will and could take other things into account. It had self determination. That magnifies, it produces added good from the performances of all of those involved with it. Now you have an entity entirely subject to individuals who are owners, or to another company, which may be publicly held. It's not that this is bad. But the presence that formerly interfused that particular public company as itself is gone. People may do the same things as before. But the circumstances in which they do them are changed. The quality of self-responsibility, and all that the philosophers know goes with that, is no more. It cannot be restored, unless by some quirk the company is promptly made public again.

Lawrence: To the same shareholders?

Michael: That's not important. To public shareholders. But under the same management, directors and officers, and with generally the same workforce. That is, the group presently imbued with the traditions that are the company's heritage as a self responsible entity.

Lawrence: You've lost me. You are trying to say something but it doesn't come out. Be specific.

Michael: I can't.

Lawrence: That means it's a shallow idea you have. There's no meat.

Michael: No, no. That means it is a new idea,

quite deep, but still new. I see many facets of it all at the same time, but there is no coherent image of it yet. My life has been logic and this is not logical. Not yet. It's an awareness of something on a different plane, an overwhelming biological and cultural event. One needs to be a poet to find the right words. It's more an intuition than an idea. A future Rousseau will tell us in penetrating detail what the modern public company is, all the relations on which it bases its justification. By then it will be more fully developed independent of government or any other central control -- unless the blight of the takeovers interferes with it.

Lawrence: Fascinating. I had no idea anyone could take a bunch of legal forms so seriously.

Michael: The large public company in all its surprising consequences may be the most important of the discoveries in man's ascent so far. The geocentric system, Darwinian biology, classical mechanics, optics, manipulation of the electromagnetic spectrum, genetic designing, all the historic advances out of man's mind. It may be the emergence of a different concept of "property", elaborated in an essential new composition, the necessary format for great groupings of humans to accomplish together inconceivable tasks that await, in the most efficient, selfless and yet individually dignified manner. It is crucial that we appreciate this masterpiece. More important than you can possibly imagine.

Why don't we just leave it at that and go on? I'm not comfortable.

Lawrence: Please. Keep talking. I know it's only stream of consciousness, but as I say I never. . .

Michael: There is a collective ideal of the established independent public company which stretches into the future, and which draws on the motives and dreams of all of those who have worked and interacted within it down through generations. Including those who also worked by only carrying on their daily functions, housework or school, as a part of a family living identified with the company.

This self-responsibility enters into everything that the company does through its agents, whether people are conscious of it or not. It comes down every chimney, in every window. We sense this spirit in any long lived organization of people in a common endeavor, but it is more pronounced in the large public company, because of the exciting mixture of capital and labor and human ingenuity, and what it is that a business enterprise does, finding and pursuing new commercial opportunities. Paradoxically it can prompt a company to opt toward better quality -- or toward bolder research, or toward a particular social benefit for its own workers or larger society -- at the deliberate and sometimes calculated expense of budgets and capital returns, temporarily or perhaps permanently.

The public company's stability, its constancy is essential for the planning and execution required of the organization of the future. Feasibility studies alone will occupy more than a whole generation. We already depend on entities capable of this steadfastness, this ability to surmount time, and that will increase.

These autonomous public corporations are infinitely preferable to government or any other sort of centralized authority over business. As time goes by they should supplant some of the functions of government, which would be good from the standpoint of our individual economic liberty.

I am saying that the sovereign public company long separated from classical ownership is an astonishing new force of a more advanced economic and social order. Probably the lead arrangement in the inevitable process of complexification. It can span a culture, and radically different cultures if need be, as can no political organization. It is situated outside both private property and public property. We could not have achieved the present standard of life without it. That is the widely held public company's bed-rock justification and it is irrefutable. For that reason alone, without considering the promise of greater things ahead, we must respect it and enhance it, study it and reform it without let-up. But not ridicule it, not constantly demean the motives of its leaders, not applaud and support those who seek to extinguish it.

The service provided to man and the potential future benefits from the widely held public company are at cross purposes with the crass, grinning egoism of the hostile takeovers. The two cannot co-exist. We have no choice. We must side with the public company. While of necessity we cannot prolong its life indefinitely, by any means, we should strive to arrange as far as possible that -- like ourselves --its destruction occurs only from causes within.

Lawrence: Are you claiming public companies necessarily do a better job than private companies?

Michael: Apples and oranges. Private companies could not have done the same job as our large public companies. The public's equity capital was essential. That's what led to the public company. That's why we have them. The sheer financial magnitude of the tasks rule out the private entrepreneur. When we begin to appreciate what else they can do it starts to become apparent that non-financial considerations also rule out the private entrepreneur in the larger undertakings.

Without owners that have a will over it, the public company is better suited to carrying out the most worthwhile initiatives of the large business enterprise. With its independence, its internalized group methods, its outside directors, its longevity, its capacity for risk and all the rest, but most of all with its very publicness, the modern public company is capable of a collective rather than an individual approach to everything it does. That makes it the more responsive to certain trends. As the predominant institution of our future, I think it may be an ideal receiver of some impulses that race through this quickening civilization we carry around with us. A means of converting them to public good. Business is in the forefront of everything in life. It shapes our political systems, our cultural pursuits, our mental habits, everything. We need to be there with the optimal pattern for progress.

The public company is also better able to reflect the dignity of one's toil in an enormous enterprise, because at all times it redounds to the credit of the institution. And those workers who depend on merit alone for employment and advancement will benefit from nothing so much as they will from the continued hegemony of large public companies in the economy.

Lawrence: It's just disjointed fluff, Michael. You mean well, but you're rambling. There's nothing solid in what you are saying.

Michael: I don't doubt that. And you demand something unquestionably solid if it's to take profits away from you.

Lawrence: What you're suggesting is that the pure company — that a bunch of forms — that it has a life of its own and that it can do some kind of good for everyone even though the people running it are bums. That there's no need to get in new top people when it's in trouble. It can just go into some kind of Zen trance and right itself.

Michael: This isn't a joking matter. I know this idea, this theory of mine seems vague to you. The most important things are impossible to define. In fact they are difficult to speak of at all. I suggest you try to see it, not sit there with a scowl on your face and defy me to open your mind to it. You have to overcome prejudices that I was never encumbered with, don't forget. You also have to overcome the unchecked dictates of your particular knack for making a great deal of money quickly.

Lawrence: People won't accept the argument that we should restrain hostile takeovers because of these shapeless notions of yours about some mystical quality inherent in public companies. You're wasting your time.

Michael: I don't put the argument that way. Hostile takeovers should be restricted for this reason: Given an opportunity like we have had in these talks, one can take all of the arguments that you can make in favor of hostile takeovers, and refute them.

Lawrence: That's your opinion.

Michael: There is nothing more to be said. You don't have a germ of a case. You just have worn out slogans, many carried over from proxy contests, all built around a fundamental anti-business theme that is trite and wrong and unfair. And a grab-bag of abuses that can all be laid at the feet of your own takeover bar. Now, over and above the emptiness of all your arguments, I have suggested for you a new dimension to the modern public company, an aspect of it you never even thought about. Admit it.

Lawrence: I do. But there are an infinity of things I never thought about. That doesn't mean they are worthwhile.

Michael: You can't dispute my idea at this point. It's too new, too basic. You don't know what to make of it.

Lawrence: I agree. I don't.

Michael: That is why the hostile takeovers should be curtailed one way or another. There is something magnificent at stake here, and we haven't figured it out yet. I say let's at least stop the takeovers until we are positive we are not wrecking something essential to our democratic society. The independent public company. A free society can drown in its own liquidity.

Takeovers will not be the only threat the large independent public company will have to face. Always there will be the dangers of excessive government intrusion into business decisions, and that includes intrusion by the courts. And of competition from state subsidized entities abroad. And there will be other dangers. We will have to address these as they arise, one at a time. The foremost problem today is takeovers.

Lawrence: Even if you are right, even if there is something more to the public company, there are thousands of public companies. Who's going to miss a handful a year? Six takeovers a year does not crumble a system. You are blowing this out of proportion.

Michael: I've tried to explain to you. Our concern must be for the potential universality of the takeover ethic. Every public company is deeply affected by every hostile takeover. This takeover mentality is right now changing attitudes within all of the public companies where they stand, even the very biggest, in a malignant way. It's like a virus and it is attacking all of them in principle. Every one of them is aware of the takeover siege. It is an inescapable distortion in their environment. As we discussed, it is no positive incentive at all, but an abusive distraction. Worse than that, it is also affirming in the bluntest way possible that society, including Federal legislators, judges and administrators, does not care at all for them and what they are, will not preserve them, does not need them, will facilitate and take satisfaction from seeing them extinguished. To me the foreseeable consequences of this will be devastating. Think what our economy, our society would be like if all our public companies practiced a new pessimism, adopted a new ethic? "Do it to yourself before they get you. Don't hope. Run scared. Trash the balance sheet. Me first. I have to protect myself. Avoid takeovers. That's the first rule." What a tragic thing it would be if our world class public companies turned into that. It would be the end of prosperity when there are still so many who have not been partaken at all. And in due time it could be the end of our political system and of our freedoms.

Lawrence: Relax. That's not going to happen. You believe public company managements are too noble to get down on that level and act that way.

Michael: It is happening right now. Public company managements have to be impressed with an instinct to maintain the company's existence. Remember, they needed that instinct in order to excel. That's where this takeover atmosphere has become a devilish counter-incentive. You know, if companies opt for self preservation first, you cannot legislate against that. You can't regulate something that subtle. There's nothing you can do. You have a nightmare.

Lawrence: Be realistic. What's the worst that can happen to the public companies? They'll disappear? We'll return to all private enterprise? No enterprise? What? What are we worried about?

Michael: I don't know. These large complex organizations of people and capital are here to stay in one form or another. It's the form that matters. They won't die out. They are growing in other countries, under different political systems. We have to focus on our system. The worst that can happen is that the status of them will change negatively. After a too lengthy existence on the rim of the takeover abyss they will become less capable, less worthy, lose all their hope, all their vitality. The managements will become utterly self-centered. At last a central authority, the government or a quasi-governmental bureau will take them all over because they have become irreparably perverted, because the ever accelerating liquidity markets were too irresponsible to be permitted any further influence in them.

Because the magnification of the individual will that is the public corporation was actually hastening our relapse to an earlier stage of development.

Call the new status socialism or utopianism or whatever you wish. We need less central government, less centralized planning of our lives more assumption of government functions by independent businesses. That's what is at stake here. That's what this takeover activity is ultimately about.

Lawrence: But you're inviting socialization of industry when you deemphasize the role of the shareholder. The shareholder is what makes the public company private property. Isn't that the surest way to keep the government's hands off it? You're backing your way into government control. If there are no true owners, the government might as well get involved.

Michael: I'm concerned about what you say. But in our constitutional history one of the earliest and most famous decisions of the Supreme Court involved the protection of a corporation —Dartmouth College — against government interference with it. The constitutional safeguards are there. But we have to be vigilant, because the form of the independent public company is still a quite fragile phenomenon. That's why I deplore the atrocity of hostile takeovers.

Lawrence: Well you can't lay socialist intentions at the doorstep of the raiders and the corporate control community. We're the spartans of free enterprise.

Michael: I know you don't see beyond the horizon of the next quick profit and I'm satisfied that's all you ever think about. But I am worried about an invisible claw that seems to be at work in all the things you folks do.

What I see is an artificial influence causing big companies to merge with even bigger companies, an increasing concentration of business that does not arise from any spontaneous business judgment or business activity. A concentration that will ease the way for a central authority to take over the control of the means of production that is American business.

And I see efforts to divorce the control of these mighty pension funds from the employer corporations that created them and the employees that are entitled to them. Just who will control them then if not some central authority?

I see efforts to get the Federal legislature and the Federal securities authorities to take full charge of matters having to do with takeovers, and to push the 50 states out of the picture entirely because their individual efforts at local regulation interfere with some national interest.

I see the most outrageous advice of the takeover bar causing even moderate Federal district judges to enter corporate boardrooms and take a seat near the head of the table.

I see compensation measures being recommended that create firestorms of public animosity toward the business class, without doing anything for takeover defense. Indeed, subverting it.

I see increasing use of expensive long term debt in takeovers, which can only represent a wish for an inflation which ruthlessly levels all private wealth and acts as a form of expropriation by any central authority.

Most of all, I see a vicious frontal attack on the motivation, the hope, the initiative and the competitive drive of the highly skilled managers of our independent public companies, on their essential talent for tackling difficult projects and getting the job done. An assault that can have no other result but to turn them all into the worst kind of bureaucratic drones and their companies into aimless wrecks that invite a stronger hand but that no one would take over —no one except a central authority that is.

When I look at all of these ostensibly uncoordinated things flowing from hostile takeovers, and also consider the added share of the burden modern business already shoulders sustaining and stabilizing our capitalist ethic and, I think, our democracy, in this age of the lessening influence of religion and of the family, when I reflect upon all of that I wonder if there isn't an unconscious purpose in this.

Read your history, Lawrence. Study the methods and the aims of socialist parties since the late 19th century. Don't make the mistake of thinking we have a social and economic system that is fixed and permanent.

Yesterday you said you were going to give me the name of a target company that was in serious difficulty.

Lawrence: I haven't had a chance to look at my files. I'll get it for you.

149

Michael: And what do we see when we look at the publicly held raiders? Over the years the performance of these companies in the stock market has been rather substandard. The acquisitions improve neither profits nor stock prices. A professor at Yale kept a score card he called the "vulture fund." Good term. Last time I heard it showed much worse results than you would expect from all these superior managers putting other managers' former assets to higher uses. Of course some Napoleonic raiders don't care about their own stock's market value, do they? They get the money out the old fashioned way — through extravagant compensation.

Lawrence: It's getting late Michael. As I look back on our talks I believe they were useful. You don't have a convert. Far from it. But you have at least cleared the air on some points where we can agree. Such as the fact that the best performing companies in the market place can also be leaders in long term R&D expenditure.

Michael: Don't assume that will continue if we maintain this takeover mentality. It won't. They know a corporate control entrepreneur would lop off that R&D in a second. To him that budget would represent interest on a potential pool of acquisition cash.

Lawrence: We have set aside junk bonds. You don't subscribe to the hysteria about them.

Michael: It's a different question, a credit question. I don't have a view on the overall level of debt. I'll leave it to others who understand that subject. My subject is hostile takeovers.

Lawrence: And poison pills, too, and golden parachutes. We agree on them, maybe for different reasons. And we both oppose government intrusion in business.

Michael: You think you oppose it. Your actions speak otherwise.

You know what the difference between us is? You would regulate some of the things the populace in Afghanistan can do in the face of a Russian invasion. No use of germs, no polluting springs, no torture. But you condone the invasion itself. You encourage it. I'm trying to stop the invasion, because its wrong. If you don't stop it, there will never be an end to the barbaric behavior it inspires, on all sides, including the middle. You'll spend all your time outlawing new practices as they appear. Until you realize that when so many effects are obnoxious, the cause itself must be obnoxious.

Lawrence: I guess in closing I think you have a one track mind on this subject. Being with you in person here I can catch your zeal and sincerity, the body language. But I'm sure anyone hearing of your views, or even reading something you might write, would not be persuaded, except for a few CEOs. There isn't anything practical in your theory of the modern public company. It's sentimental mush. We're talking about business. Business is tough. As for your animosity toward takeovers you're just another one of those people who stand beside history asking it to "stop."

Michael: I want it to keep going because it's going well. You're the one who is stopping a process.

I also want to ask something of you. We both desire the right thing in the long run. In your larger arbitrage you are only borrowing all those portfolio profits you and your pals make. I'm not going to write you off because this voyage we are on together is too wonderful and you're going to be converted sooner or later. Pretend you are out of the market, and think more about the nature of a public company, will you do that? Think about the enormous good they do. Try to see how important they have been in this century to our economic and social development. And that has been largely without benefit of the unique and invaluable insights that women are just now contributing to corporate activity in ever growing numbers. Extrapolate the principal technological and cultural trends you see in our society today, and try to imagine how we can progress in the future without an even greater dependence on the special genius of the independent public company. If you'll do that, this has been worthwhile.

Lawrence: I will.

APPENDIX

Prominent Uninvited Cash Tender Offers — 1977–1987

DATE	TARGET	BIDDER	RESULT (HIGH BID)
3/77	Babcock & Wilcox	United Technologies	After protracted litigation, B&W became a division of McDermott Incorporated. ($750 M.)
11/77	Carborundum	Eaton Corporation	After brief litigation, Carborundum became a division of Kennecott Corporation. ($567 M.)
6/78	Pet Inc.	IC Industries	Pet became a division of IC. ($375 M.)
9/78	Carrier Corporation	United Technologies	After protracted litigation, Carrier became a division of Technologies. ($950 M.)

DATE	TARGET	BIDDER	RESULT (HIGH BID)
11/78	P.R. Mallory	Dart Industries	Mallory became a division of Dart. ($258 M.)
1/79	McGraw-Hill	American Express	Offer was withdrawn by American Express before it was actually made, AMEX protesting that it assumed McGraw-Hill management would be receptive to an offer, or else it never would have been announced in the first place. ($1 B.)
4/79	F.W. Woolworth	Brascan	Brascan bid was made to dissuade bid by Bronfman interests for control of Brascan itself. The Bronfmans eventually got control of Brascan and stopped the proposed offer before it was officially made. (Prior to the Brascan

DATE	TARGET	BIDDER	RESULT (HIGH BID)
			cancellation, a banker for Woolworth testified in South Carolina that he had been authorized to find a higher bidder for Woolworth. ($1.1 B))
10/79	ERC	Connecticut General	After protracted litigation, ERC became a divison of Getty Oil. ($570 M.)
3/80	Liggett Group	Grand Metroplitan	After protracted litigation, Liggett became a division of Grand Met. ($570 M.)
7/80	Pullman Inc.	McDermott Incorporated	After protracted litigation, Pullman became a division of Wheelabrator–Frye. ($600 M.)
9/80	Crouse–Hinds	Intcrnorth	After protracted litigation, Crouse–Hinds became a division of Cooper Industries. ($720 M.)

DATE	TARGET	BIDDER	RESULT (HIGH BID)
3/81	St. Joe Minerals	Seagram	After protracted litigation, St. Joe became a division of Fluor. ($2.6 B.)
6/81	Conoco	Seagrams	After protracted litigation, Conoco became a division of DuPont. ($6.82 B.)
6/81	Texasgulf	Elf Aquitaine	Texasgulf became a division of Elf. ($2.74 B.)
7/81	Connecticut General REIT	British National Coal Board	After protracted litigation, Conn. Gen. REIT became a division of Prudential Insurance. ($340 M.)
9/81	Sunbeam Corp.	IC Industries	After protracted litigation, Sunbeam became a division of Allegheny International. ($528 M.)
9/81	Grumman	LTV Corp.	As a result of antitrust litigation by Grumman, LTV was enjoined and withdrew its offer. ($642 M.)

DATE	TARGET	BIDDER	RESULT (HIGH BID)
10/81	Marathon Oil	Mobil	After protracted litigation, Marathon became a division of U.S. Steel. ($6.2 B.)
1/82	Brunswick Corp	Whittaker Corp.	Whittaker withdrew after Brunswick sold its key, non-cyclical medical unit to American Home Products. Brunswick's CEO resigned 2 months later. ($600 M.)
3/82	Joseph Schlitz Brewing Co.	Stroh Brewing Co.	After brief litigation, Schlitz became a division of Stroh. ($316 M.)
6/82	Cities Service	Mesa Petroleum Co.	After protracted litigation, and an abortive $4.8B acquisition agreement with Gulf Oil, Cities Service became a division of Occidental Petroleum Corporation. ($4 B.)
8/82	Martin Marietta Corporation	Bendix Corporation	After protracted litigation, and a bid by Martin for a majority of Bendix, Allied Corporation

DATE	TARGET	BIDDER	RESULT (HIGH BID)
			acquired Bendix for $1.9B and Martin remained independent, but with 39% of its stock owned by Allied and $400M in equity (down from $1.2B.)
12/82	El Paso Company	Burlington Northern Inc.	After brief litigation, El Paso became a division of Burlington. ($516 M.)
12/82	General American Oil Company of Texas	Mesa Petroleum	General American became a division of Phillips Petroleum Co. ($1.14B.)
6/83	Lenox Inc.	Brown-Forman Distillers Corp.	After brief litigation, Lenox became a division of Brown-Forman. ($427 M.)
6/83	Texas Gas Resources Corporation	Coastal Corporation	Texas Gas became a division of CSX. ($1.1 B.)
12/83	Getty Oil Co.	Pennzoil Co.	Getty became a division of Texaco. ($10 B.)

DATE	TARGET	BIDDER	RESULT (HIGH BID)
1/84	Houston Natural Gas Corporation	Coastal Corporation	After brief litigation and a $900 M bid by Houston for all of Coastal, Coastal withdrew its offer, as did Houston, in return for $42.1 M "peace payment" by Houston and a 5 year put to Houston of about one-fourth of Coastal's gas production at a 30% premium over the price of regulated gas. ($1.3 B.)
2/84	Gulf Oil	Mesa Petroleum Co.	Gulf became a division of Standard Oil Co. of California. ($13.4 B.)
4/84 and 11/86	Carter Hawley Hale Stores	The Limited and DiBartolo	CCH became 47.3% owned by General Cinema.
11/84	Prentice-Hall	Gulf & Western	Prentice-Hall became a division of Gulf & Western. ($695 M.)
12/84	Scovill	First City Properties	Scovill became a division of First City Properties. ($516 M.)

DaTE	TARGET	BIDDER	RESULT (HIGH BID)
12/84	Phillips Petroleum	Icahn Group	After protected litigation involving first Pickens and then Icahn, Phillips did a debt-for-equity exchange offer resulting in an inversion of its debt to equity ratio and a 38% decrease in proforma income.
3/85	American Natural	Coastal	ANR became a division of Coastal. ($2.5 B.)
4/85	Uniroyal, Inc.	Robin Acquisition Corp. (Carl Icahn)	Uniroyal became a division of a private company. ($836 M.)
4/85	Unocal	Mesa Partners II	Unocal did a debt-for-equity exchange offer resulting in an inversion of its debt to equity ratio and a 33% decrease in proforma net income.
4/85	Crown Zellerbach Corp.	General Oriental Securities Ltd. (Sir James Goldsmith)	Crown became a majority owned subsidiary of General Oriental.
5/85	AMF	Minstar, Inc. (Irwin Jacobs)	AMF became a division of Minstar. ($632 M.)

DATE	TARGET	BIDDER	RESULT (HIGH BID)
5/85	Trans World Airlines, Inc.	Carl Icahn	TWA became a majority owned subsidiary of Icahn. ($795 M.)
5/85	Revlon, Inc.	Pantry Pride	After brief litigation, Revlon became a division of Pantry Pride. ($2.2 B.)
8/85	SCM Corp.	Hanson Trust PLC	After brief litigation, SCM became a division of Hanson Trust. ($911 M.)
9/85	Richardson-Vicks Inc.	Unilever N.V.	After brief litigation, Richardson-Vicks became a division of Procter & Gamble. ($1.24 B.)
10/85	Pacific Lumber	Maxxam Group	Pacific Lumber became a division of Maxxam. ($870 M.)
10/85	Cluett-Peabody	Paul Bilzerian	After brief litigation, Cluett-Peabody became a division of West Point Pepperell. ($375 M.)

DATE	TARGET	BIDDER	RESULT (HIGH BID)
10/85	Hoover Co.	Chicago Pacific	Hoover Co. became a division of Chicago Pacific. ($533 M.)
10/85	Transway International	Nortek Inc.	After brief litigation, Transway became a division of International Controls Corp. ($322 M.)
10/85	Southland Royalty	Burlington Northern	Southland Royalty became a division of Burlington Northern. ($715 M.)
10/85	Potlatch	Belzbergs	Offer was withdrawn by Belzberg's before it was actually made, when Potlatch repurchased Belzberg's stake. No litigation filed by Potlatch and suggestions that Belzberg offer was proposed to prompt a buyback.
12/85	Midcon Corp.	Wagner & Brown, Freeport McMoran	Midcon became a division of Occidental Petroleum ($3 B.)

DATE	TARGET	BIDDER	RESULT (HIGH BID)
2/86	White Consolidated	AB Electrolux	White Consolidated became a division of Electrolux. ($742 M.)
5/86	Sperry Corp.	Burroughs	Sperry became a division of Burroughs. ($4.4 B.)
5/86	Saga Corp.	Marriott	Saga became a division of Marriott. ($502 M.)
5/86	John Blair & Co.	McFadden Holdings	Blair became a division of Reliance Capital. ($250 M.)
6/86	Associated Dry Goods	May Department Stores	Associated Dry Goods became a division of May. ($2.5 B.)
6/86	Sanders Associates	Loral Corp.	Sanders became a division of Lockheed. ($1.8 B.)
6/86	Fruehauf Corp.	Asher Edelman	Fruehauf became a division of Merrill Lynch. ($1.4 B.)
7/86	Hammermill Paper	Paul Bilzerian	Hammermill became a division of International Paper. ($1.1 B.)

DATE	TARGET	BIDDER	RESULT (HIGH BID)
7/86	NL Industries	Harold Simmons	NL became a majority owned subsidiary of Simmons. ($450 M.)
8/86	Ex-Cell-O	Textron	Ex-Cell-O became a division of Textron. ($1.05 B.)
8/86	Owens-Corning Fiberglas Corp.	Wickes Cos.	Owens-Corning did a debt-for-equity exchange resulting in more than an inversion of its debt to equity ratio and more than 100% reduction in proforma net income.
9/86	Ryan Homes, Inc.	NV Homes LP	Ryan became a division of NV Homes. ($312 M.)
11/86	Gillette Co.	Revlon Group Inc.	Revlon's 14% stake was repurchased, resulting in a doubling of Gillette's debt.

DATE	TARGET	BIDDER	RESULT (HIGH BID)
11/86	Chesebrough-Ponds	American Brands	Chesebrough-Ponds became a division of Unilever. ($3.1B)
11/86	Lane Co.	Interco	Lane became a division of Interco.($487.5 M.)
11/86	Joy Manufacturing Co.	Pullman-Peabody Co.	Joy Manufacturing became a division of a private company. ($620 M.)
2/87	Cyclops Corp.	Audio/Video Affiliates, Inc. and Citicorp Capital Investment Ltd.	Cyclops became a division of Dixons Group PLC. ($393 M.)
2/87	ChemLawn Corp.	Waste Management Inc.	ChemLawn became a division of Ecolab. ($370 M.)
3/87	GenCorp.	AFG Industries Inc. and Wagner & Brown	After protracted litigation, GenCorp repurchased 54% of its shares, inverting its debt to equity ratio.

INDEX

www.ingramcontent.com/pod-product-compliance
Lightning Source LLC
Chambersburg PA
CBHW021541200526
45163CB00014B/722